Riding In Africa

Riding In Africa

Ian Williams

iUniverse, Inc.
New York Lincoln Shanghai

Riding In Africa

Copyright © 2005 by Ian Hugh Williams

iUniverse books may be ordered through booksellers or by contacting:

iUniverse
2021 Pine Lake Road, Suite 100
Lincoln, NE 68512
www.iuniverse.com
1-800-Authors (1-800-288-4677)

ISBN-13: 978-0-595-37301-7 (pbk)
ISBN-13: 978-0-595-81699-6 (ebk)
ISBN-10: 0-595-37301-1 (pbk)
ISBN-10: 0-595-81699-1 (ebk)

Printed in the United States of America

DEDICATION

"Oh no, I've killed my husband."

"Of the gladdest moments, methinks, in human life, is the departing upon a distant journey into unknown lands. Shaking off with one effort the fetters of Habit—the leaden weight of Routine—the cloak of carking Care, and the slavery of Home—man feels once more happy. The blood flows with the fast circulation of youth, excitement gives new vigour to the muscles, and a sense of sudden freedom adds an inch to the stature. Afresh dawns the morn of life, again the bright world is beautiful to the eye, and the glorious face of nature gladdens the soul. A journey in fact, appeals to Imagination, to Memory, to Hope—the sister Graces of our moral being."

—Richard Francis Burton in "Zanzibar; City Island and Coast"

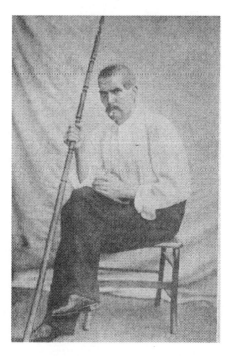

Richard Burton in his tent in Africa
(from Life of Sir Richard Burton, by Isabel Burton)

DISCLAIMER

I have always liked Evelyn Waugh's disclaimer in Brideshead Revisited:

"I am not I; thou art not he or she; they are not they."

However, I am I, you probably are he or she, and they are most certainly they. The names, with one or two exceptions where people actually managed to come out of these stories with some shred of dignity intact, have been changed to protect the guilty. If you recognize yourself please contact my attorney. This reminds me to stick with the old Arab proverb:

"Speak the truth with one foot in the stirrup."

The air of heaven is that which blows between a horse's ears.

—Arab proverb

Contents

Illustrations

Photographs, often taken by the author from the back of a horse, provide the inspiration for some of the line drawings found through out the book. Here is an example of an original photograph.

Photo taken whilst riding

Map of Safaris

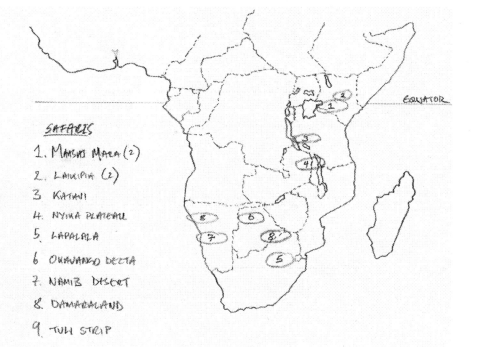

SAFARIS

1. MAASAI MARA (2)
2. LAIKIPIA (2)
3. KATAVI
4. NYIKA PLATEAU
5. LAPALALA
6. OKAVANGO DELTA
7. NAMIB DESERT
8. DAMARALAND
9. TULI STRIP

Preface

I nearly died in Africa in 2004, something I would have deemed incredible in 1994. This book tells the story of how I came to be in Africa. It is a story of horses, people and the magic, power and excitement of Africa. Africa pulls on my very genes. It does this through a heady mixture of sights, sounds and smells that invigorate me as nothing else can. I am sure that being on horseback opened my spirit to the essence of Africa. It rendered me vulnerable and took away any pretense at competence or the other myriad things we use to seal ourselves off from what the world is telling us. It was in this vulnerable state that I first went to Africa and let it make its mark on me. My experiences were humbling in the sense of its Latin root, *humus* meaning ground. I became grounded in Africa.

My story starts with my near death and then looks back over the previous decade at the experiences and events that brought me to that close encounter. This is not a travelogue, but rather what I hope is an amusing canter through many aspects of African flora, fauna, language, customs, and above all people, primarily seen from the back of a horse.

1

Running out of Gas on Mount Kenya

"He looked about him with weak desperation for comfort, someone to touch him other than medically, remembering the clasp of the Negro's hand in the ambulance—and not finding it."

—Paula Fox "Poor George"

I never thought I would die in Africa. On reflection, that's not true. A lot of the time I was in Africa I thought I could very well die there, especially when I was on horseback, and yet the time when I came closest to death did not happen on horseback. It started on a horse, with a three-hour ride through the ranches of Laikipia at the foot of Mount Kenya in February of 2004, but ended two and a half weeks later as I boarded a South African Airway's flight from Nairobi to Johannesburg with a chit for oxygen in my hand and my wife, Nancy, pushing my wheelchair.

This was our second safari in Laikipia, the first being in 2002. On the first night of the safari, after a three-hour ride to get used to the horses, we were sitting at the dinner table. We were in the bush enjoying the warm evening and the sounds of insects clicking, buzzing, and chirping in the trees. Timothy, the headwaiter, came out and placed Bakelite plates in front of us. They were a mixture of red and green that I remember from so many Kenyan safaris. The candlelight lit up acacia branches that hung over the table casting generous shadows on my riding companions as we drank and talked of the coming days. I was feeling fine and chatting to a newfound friend about her life in New York. As the evening progressed, I started to feel unwell. I could not specifically say what was wrong but I stopped drinking, a sure sign of a very serious problem. About halfway though dinner I started to feel cold; the sensation was that of a plug being pulled from the center of my body and all my heat draining out. I excused myself from dinner and went back to the tent where I started to experience paroxysms of shaking. The nights can be chilly in the Kenya highlands and in a somewhat quaint, if sexist, tradition, all the women guests get hot water bottles put in their sleeping bags during dinner. I grabbed Nancy's hot water bottle and clutched it to my chest but just could not stop the shaking. Eventually I fell asleep only to wake with a fit of violent coughing, a cycle that was repeated throughout the night.

The next day I felt bad, not bad enough to need medical care, but enough so that I couldn't contemplate riding. I received sage advice along the lines of "You are just going to have to sweat it out." One old Africa hand told me to do what he does and get one of the staff to make me a hot toddy of honey and whiskey and I'd be fine. I passed the day in a state of suspended animation. I couldn't read and could barely move. I had a little soup for lunch but that was it. I simply sat in front of the tent and stared into the middle distance.

That night was worse, my lungs really hurt and I had to sit up every hour to cough to relieve them. The next day everyone went for an early ride. All I could do was get to the camp chair in front of the tent and sit. When they returned I could not move, I tried to stand up and just crumpled on the floor. A radiologist on the trip was concerned that I might be dehydrated and said I needed medical attention. Our guide, Mark, found an expired saline drip intended for horses and the radiologist managed to get it into my arm.

Mark said there was a cottage hospital in the nearby town of Nanyuki where he had had good experience in the past. At this stage, I think everyone felt I had some sort of acute infection and that I would be back in no time. Mark went on to encourage me by speaking well of the doctor at Nanyuki Hospital, one Dr Butt. He told the story of the time when Tristan, the owner of the safari outfit we were riding with, was leading a ride and one of the grooms fell off his horse and cut his ear badly. Tristan, in typical fashion, told him not to make a fuss and get back on the horse. It was only when the other riders complained that the ear looked bad, and was in fact "hanging off", that Tristan relented and took him to Nanyuki Hospital and the tender ministrations of Dr. Butt.

With this glorious testimony ringing in my ears (as it were) Nancy and I were driven for two hours across the Laikipia plains to Nanyuki Cottage hospital. Land Rover trips through the bush are seldom what they appear on television. The holes are enormous and numerous and in this case the area was not well traveled so there wasn't actually much of a road for the first hour or so. My expired saline drip hung from a hook in the Land Rover and I felt distinctly unwell as we bounced and jolted our way to Nanyuki. We drove through the center of town. The hustle and bustle of people walking, and carrying all sorts of strange loads filled the place with an energy. There were impromptu markets and groups of people standing under trees, talking, roasting maize, or simply watching. The red shukas or cloaks of the Maasai punctuated the scene as they cajoled herds of goats and cattle along the grass at the roadside. A coat of dust settled over everything. The smell is distinctive. It is a fusion of sweat, dust, and wood smoke. It causes a tinny taste in my mouth and I love it. However, on this particular occasion, none of this color gave me much heart.

We turned off the main road onto a long dirt track. My first impression of Nanyuki Cottage Hospital was a dazzling collection of white buildings with nurses in, what looked like 50's-style, starched uniforms.

A nurse came out to meet me and ushered me to a private room on the second floor. The hospital did not have an elevator and I climbed a flight of concrete steps. I did not think I was going to make it and by the time I reached the top, I was ready to drop. I received a private room just because I was white. Had I been black I am sure that I would have been in a ward on the first floor. I was grateful, in spite of the climb, but couldn't help thinking of the irony. It was 40 years after Kenya's independence from Britain and yet here was this old Brit getting special treatment. It may have been because I could obviously pay; otherwise, I wouldn't be riding around Africa on a horse. I like to think it was this that marked me for the private room and not my skin color.

The room I entered looked like an English working class bedroom of the 1950s. The Sister, Lucy Wamsiro, came in and hooked me up to a monitor. Lucy was tall with dark black skin and high cheekbones. She had a presence about her and exuded confidence and compassion in equal measure. My heart rate was 160 and my blood oxygen concentration was 80, normal would be nearly 100. Dr. Butt came in; he was a handsome man in his forties, with a round head and a centered stance. As with many other doctors we would encounter he was Indian. He gave me the once over and quickly diagnosed advanced bilateral pneumonia and put me on oxygen as well as calling the Flying Doctor to take me to Nairobi. By this time, I was drifting in and out of consciousness and it was all I could do to lie on the bed and breathe. Lisa, one of our riding group, and a registered nurse, had come with Nancy and me to the hospital to provide some moral support and she sat by my bed trying to encourage us. "Do you have an EKG?" she asked. "Well, yes, but it is a bit old." replied Dr. Butt. The EKG was exhumed from God knows where but its plug would not fit into any of the sockets in the room. Lisa's smile faded a little and she turned her attention to the machine monitoring my blood pressure and oxygen concentration.

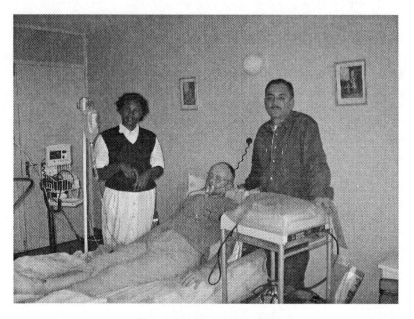

Sister Wamsiro and Dr. Butt

Nancy had gone to see about the bill and Lisa and I were alone in the room. All of a sudden, there was a scrabbling thud and we looked to see a red hornbill beating its wings against the window. The bird had a long red beak and large black eyes set in white cheeks. The window was open and the hornbill quickly flew in and out of the room. "That must be an omen" said Lisa, clearly disturbed, and we both looked at the window in silence. It is strange how things like that take on an aura of emotion and superstition, especially if you are sick.

When Dr. Butt said he was calling the Flying Doctors I felt a quiver of excitement. I had heard of them as a boy and the idea of flying with them thrilled me, even as I struggled for my breath. To meet the plane we had to get to Nanyuki's landing strip and the hospital ambulance was pressed into service. This was a small white Toyota pick-up with a cap, into the back of which a mattress had been thrown. The inside of the pickup was stifling and I began for the first time to think this isn't Kansas. In spite of the small space in climbed a nurse who proceeded to take my blood pressure every 5 minutes and a male orderly who held my leg with a firm pressure and gave me great comfort. His was a simple act of kindness, unasked for, and given without conscious thought. As Leo Buscaglia said, "Too often we underestimate the power of a touch, a smile, a kind word, a listening ear, an honest compliment, or the smallest act of caring, all of which have the potential to turn a life around." I think that man turned my life around and I don't even know his name.

I lay in the back of the pickup on the dirt strip waiting for the sound of the plane's engine, and after about 20 minutes there it came, what a relief. There is no sweeter sound than that when standing on some dirt landing strip in the middle of nowhere. This time was no different from all the others when I have stared into the vast blue and strained to catch that throb. In 2003 AMREF carried out 550 evacuations from the bush, I was now part of the 2004 statistic.

As the plane taxied to a halt next to the ambulance I could see, painted on the side, an inscription that read "Donated by the people of the Netherlands." I later learned that my dear Dutch friend Gerry Briels had made a contribution to the Flying Doctors; later when he heard of my escapade he said he wished he had stipulated it was not to be used to ferry bloody Brits around Africa! Fifty-five minutes later—after flying through low-hanging black clouds and rain with Mount Kenya looming through the cabin windows, we emerged into the sunlight and Nairobi's Wilson airport. After we landed, I was taken off the plane and put in the back of a waiting ambulance.

We inched our way through the traffic to Nairobi hospital and as the doors of the ambulance opened, I saw three nurses waiting for me. They moved me onto a gurney and wheeled me into the hospital. I was trundled down cream walled corridors and then pushed through black rubber swing doors into the ER. There were four beds, three had dark green curtains around them, and I could hear people groaning inside. I was lifted onto the bed and Dr. Patel appeared. He was a coolly competent man whose specialty was the cardiovascular system. As I lay there, the nurses pulled off my clothes and everyone seemed to be looking at the monitor above my head that read out my heart rate, blood pressure, and oxygen concentration. The whole place seemed dark and small. Dr. Moniz, an anesthesiologist, joined Dr. Patel and together they confirmed Dr. Butt's diagnosis of pneumonia. A mobile X-ray machine appeared in the small emergency room, and showed the pneumonia to be severe in both lungs. I had only 15% of my total lung capacity; this was so poor that Dr. Patel wanted to put me on a respirator to help me breathe. There was no way I was going to allow this to happen. When I was quite small, I remembered seeing a program on the BBC about a terminal cancer patient. I vividly recalled the scene in which the doctor said to the patient that he needed to go on a ventilator and that once this happened he would not come off it. I can see the anguish in the man's face even today as he confronted his imminent death. In my distress, I obscured the difference between a ventilator and a respirator and I was not going to let them take this first step to finishing me off. Unbeknownst to me Dr. Patel and Moniz gave me some morphine and while I was "otherwise" occupied, they intubated me for the respirator and put a venous catheter into my superior vena cava for the administration of i.v. drugs. This was also used to measure my cardiac venous pressure, which was very high because I was starting to go into congestive heart failure.

My next stop was the ICU. As in hospitals the world over it was the noisiest place I had ever been. I think this is because my body yearned for silence so that it could focus on repairing itself and any noise was a distraction.

Nancy kept a journal of all that happened. It is a raw account of her experiences and I quote portions of it here verbatim.

> *Resuscitation, Observation and Procedures. Luckily, we are going to Observation. Two forms to fill out—one for admittance, later, one for the ICU. After Dr. Patel comes, blood is drawn; Ian is wheeled to the ICU. I must pay, KS5000 is required—luckily, MasterCard is accepted. I hurriedly sign the slip and proceed with Ian to the ICU. I am shepherded to the waiting room. There is a large Indian family sitting in the chairs, a banal TV show in American accents playing. A flower arrangement of carnations is next to me…pink and white with some other small white flower on a white metal stand. I hate carnations…funerals in Illinois…everyone standing around making polite small talk…the smell of carnations and formalin.*

> *I break down. I can't hold back any longer. The tears flow, I am shaking. I had survived the trip to observation, X-ray and here now that we were at a standstill I could not hold back. Suddenly a very pretty middle-aged woman in a sari put her arms around me to comfort me. She was so calm, so beautiful. She said I was to put everything into god's hands and I was to be strong. She asked where I was staying and if I needed a ride—should she leave her number? I said, foolishly perhaps, that I would be fine…I was brought back to Ian's private room in the ICU. He was connected to an i.v. drip of amiodorone and had a mask for O_2. His heart rate was still in the 140s to 150s and he was in atrial fibrillation.*

It is seven. I go back in, they have forgotten me. Ian is on the respirator. Tears are pooling in his eyes. I say its OK, its OK and gently wipe them. The sister holds his hand. "You will be fine, you will be fine." His pO₂ is 98, HR 148. The pulmonologist explains they have him lightly sedated and have paralyzed him so that he is completely relaxed and can let the respirator breathe for him. One of the nurses asks me to take a BG (blood glucose). I load the glucometer and stick Ian's finger but I am shaking too much, it doesn't work. Dr. Patel said, "The nurses should be doing this. You are shaking, are you OK? Sit down" I sit down; I am scared. The sight of Ian flat out on a respirator, so helpless is terrifying. My god! Dr. Patel says it is difficult to see this when it is someone you know. The respiration rate is 19, pO₂ 98; HR 142. "I would be happier if the heart rate was lower." Dr. Patel said. He stands with us for 15 minutes. Everything is stable, the sister tells me to go home. There is a vice around my heart, I feel I can't breathe.

Thanks to the help of Tristan and his wife, Cindy, Nancy had a room in the Serena Hotel, which was about 5 miles from the hospital. I was worried about Nancy traveling after dark in Nairobi, but the ward Sister called a taxi and made the driver come into the ward for her inspection. His name was Patrick Ndolo Mutisya. This kind and gentle man became Nancy's driver and our friend for the time I was in hospital. It made me feel so much better knowing that she was safe with him.

During the night, I pulled the respirator out much to Dr. Moniz' distress. Fortunately, he decided that I could get by without it and did not try to re-intubate me. The next day I gained an impression of my room and the hospital. The floors were squeaky-clean linoleum and polished within an inch of their lives. The windows had steel frames and worn brass handles which closed onto a tongued latch, just like the council house I lived in when I was 5 years old. As I lay in bed, I could hear the gentle tapping of workmen in the hospital courtyard lifting and relaying brick. On the other side of the courtyard was the hospital laundry. It was a mass of pipes and steam like something out of Victorian England, with all the sheets hung out on lines to dry.

My room in the ICU had some odd, non-descript 1960s style curtains separating it from the next. The pattern on the curtain was of pale blue, pale gold and coral vertical stripes. That evening, I saw writ large on these curtains the whole panoply of hell. As my eye followed a particular stripe down, its tone and texture changed and faces would emerge: Marilyn Monroe; Joseph Conrad; Lenin, Claudette Colbert. Some not known, others realized as ciphers walking down the road. I am sure some innocent journeyman designer came up with the pattern, but my condition and drugs transformed it into a tableau that Bosch would stand in awe of.

At night, I had the most horrendous dreams. I could see in my mind's eye intricately carved, interlocking tree roots that formed faces. As I looked at them under a pale, self-generated searchlight, the eyes of the faces closed, the roots moved and I encountered another face and another pair of eyes that looked at me balefully. These eyes closed in turn as the face folded in on itself, back into the mass of tree roots. The whole sense was one of seething movement in which faces would emerge for a moment to engage me with their stare and then disappear back in on themselves. Suddenly a dark, blood red viscous liquid with black swirls replaced the tree roots, and the faces began to form again in this slow moving black marbled blood, appearing and disappearing with the same tempo as before.

Throughout this experience, I felt very conscious. I was watching what is, or what would be. As if the ghost of Christmas future had taken me into the nether world and shown me what was there.

The worst vision was of a rock face in which faces bristling with guns protruded from crevices in the stones. Slowly the rock collapsed in on itself and the faces disappeared, only to be replaced by new, anxious visages looking out from the rock with guns at the ready. I was sure I was watching the souls of those who had recently died enter the underworld and squeeze those already there so that the latter dissolved and the new ones took their place for a brief moment. The look on those faces was one of needing to be seen and noticed by beings like me, who were on the banks of the Styx.

On other occasions the scene would be brighter with more light and then flecks of black would appear like blood cells flowing in jerky movements. Holes appeared revealing tunnels of light, which pulled my gaze into them. For some reason my body did not move towards them. I cannot tell if I pulled this vision from my subconscious where it was stored after reading and hearing so much about near death experiences in which many people claim to see these tunnels of light or whether this was new for me.

As an aside, this is a very important question. I am neither religious nor especially spiritual. I do not believe in an after life, although I dearly like the idea of karma and re-incarnation. My own view of re-incarnation is that following our death we live on as the memories and experiences we have given others. Sometimes, our impact has been so seminal that people who did not know us when we were alive come across our legacy in our writings, thoughts, or ideas, often contained and expressed by other people. In this sense, no matter who we were, nor what we did, no matter how humble and modest our sphere of influence was we are re-incarnated. The stronger our presence whilst alive, the longer our karma endures.

I cannot be certain that what I saw in my dreams was in any way "real" or whether it was, instead, simply my brain's rehash of stories, told and written in human history for thousands of years. Perhaps it is our collective yearning for something after death, which perpetuates this "myth", such that those who stand on the brink naturally "see" this image and report it back on their return from the abyss and so reinforce the mythology.

On top of all this, it is hard to sort out the effects of morphine from those of a near death experience. I am sure it was a combination of both. Whilst what I have just written is my best recollection of what was happening inside my head, here is how I appeared to the outside world as recorded by Nancy.

> *2:00 p.m. HR 153, RR 42, pO2 93. Tazxocin, Cipro, Digitalis 2.5 mg, low dose morphine. We do Ian's blood glucose, it is 173 mg/dl and we have to calculate it in millimolar—the sister uses a calculator and says 9.6 mM. I say that seems high. Ian points a finger and says, "Nancy 173 mg/dl is 9.6 mM. How dumb can you get?"*
>
> *"You are quite enjoying this Nancy, you like to tell me to drink my tea." "Richard is on the phone—he wants to talk to me."—snapping his fingers.*
> *"There are two parallel universes I have been going back and forth between the two."*
> *"If I die, its her fault." Laughing pointing to me.*
> *Ian asking for cold water. When he received about 25ml, he said "Thank you very much, that made me feel so much better!"*
>
> *"To help the doctor cut it up out of the freezer."*
> *"What?"*
> *"The ice cream."*
> *"I am sure this is how Einstein discovered relativity I mean insulin, discovered…"*
> *"God bless you Nancy."*
> *"We're going to do this."*
> *"Are we about to head out?"*
> *"Are we having dinner here?"*
> *"I want some ambien to sleep", feigning writing, "Get me a scrip."*

"I just left some fat Germans and they had a black mamba brought by Steve Rufus"
Looking at his arm, "I have a manifold here."

It was now my second day in the hospital and I did not respond to the combinations of antibiotics and antitvirals they had given me. At about this time things began to look grim.

They may indeed have been grim for me but they were grimmer for Nancy. We had always jokingly said that if we died in Africa we would like to be chucked out to the hyenas and recycled into the soil of our roots. This was starting to look a lot less like a joke now. What would Nancy do with me? She could have me flown back to America, but why bother? It seemed like such a waste of resources only to have my corpse burned in Connecticut and my ashes scattered on the waters of Long Island Sound where I have spent so many hours rowing. Perhaps Nancy could persuade our guide, Mark, to tie me to the top of a Land Rover and drive me out into the Maasai Mara.

For reasons that aren't entirely clear to me, even today, the doctors decided to try the antibiotic vancomycin as a last resort. I started to respond. My breathing eased and after a while, the doctors decided that I could move out of the ICU into the HDU (high dependency unit). Ironically, this was probably my worst time. The ward was open and everyone around me seemed to be throwing up, experiencing diarrhea or shouting, often simultaneously. My bed was at the end of the ward next to two private rooms. In one was a woman with some immune suppression problems such that everyone who went in had to wear a mask, and next to her was a man with a brain tumor waiting for an operation. He was white and kept making racist remarks to the black staff. They tolerated this and forgave him these outbursts with a dignity that was admirable. The ward was very noisy and I simply could not sleep. People were being wheeled in and out throughout the day and night. Relatives would file in and stand around the beds like Greek choruses, distraught and not knowing what to do or say as the patients were often too ill to talk. Because I was feeling better, I was more aware of all these comings and goings and so I could not sleep. Exhaustion began to make me feel low.

It was in the HDU that I took my first walk after having arrived in the hospital. My physiotherapist, Esther, decided that I would benefit from a brief stagger up and down the ward. I put on my shorts, and with my hospital gown hitched up, I walked around looking rather like Gandhi. I was the source of some considerable entertainment for the other patients in the ward since I had an i.v. in each arm and was non-too sure footed.

After a couple of sleepless days and nights in the HDU I managed to persuade Dr. Muhindi, my pulmonary doctor, that I really didn't need the round the clock surveillance in which the HDU specialized so well. I also found out that there were private rooms in the hospital. I asked about them and a nurse produced a list. There must have been twenty different categories. I thought for about three seconds and decided that I would gladly mortgage my house to get somewhere I could sleep, so I chose the most expensive room.

Kim—a male nurse in the HDU—pushed my wheel chair to the North Wing. As he pushed me, he whispered in my ear that the room I was going to was where the President stayed when he came to hospital. Kim, who was a Kikuyu, was very smart and articulate. He talked of his optimism for President Kabeki (also a Kikuyu) and contrasted him with the former president, Daniel arap Moi who was Kalenjin. Kim told me how in Moi's time in the 1990's, because of government corruption and skimming of public monies there was no refuse system and a huge pile of garbage built up on Moi Avenue in the center of Nairobi.

DANIEL ARAP MOI'S BEDROOM

As Kim pushed me into the private wing of the hospital, it was like entering an English Norman church folded into the Cotswold Hills. The silence of the room was astonishing and deafening. I felt energy flow through my body. It was similar to doing the plough in yoga and feeling the initial pain dissolve as the endorphins ooze out from the stretched nerves. Nancy helped me to disconnect the infusion lines in both my arms and I turned on my stomach, she reconnected them and I fell into a deep sleep. All I could hear was the soft gurgling of the water in my oxygen mask and birds singing in the trees outside the window. This was the turning point for me. It was a strange feeling to be lying in bed knowing that Daniel arap Moi had lain there.

The room was large, perhaps thirty feet by forty feet with its own bathroom, which, in turn, was some fifteen foot square. Along one side of the room was a picture window, which looked out over the hospital gardens. Large trees pushed their branches towards the window. There was a standing water pipe in the garden with an old brass spigot from which gardeners would periodically fill dented zinc buckets. The rhythm of their work gave me a sense of well-being. Beyond the garden was the busy Ngong Road continually flowing with traffic and people walking back and forth. I spent many hours looking out on this scene as my lungs healed.

Hizi Ndizo Dawa Zako

Like so many British school children of my time, I specialized academically at a very early age. I enjoyed my last history, geography, art, and English literature classes when I was 14. After that, I delved into the hard sciences, math, physics, and chemistry. Biology at the time was a halfway house into science for dummies. Because of this enlightened philosophy, I left school being able to solve differential equations, manipulate imaginary numbers, and determine the composition of any number of white colorless crystals using Holmesian logic and chemical analysis. Yet, I had almost no survival skills, no insight into the world of poetry and literature and little understanding of the political world. I went to university and eventually earned a Ph. D. in biochemistry, which introduced me to the woman I would marry. She took me to America, which landed me in Pfizer as a research scientist in their laboratories in southeast Connecticut.

I joined Pfizer in 1981 when no one had heard of it. If I met someone at a party and they asked me what I did they would look askance and then drift off, having assessed me as a waif on the professional circuit of life. How times change. With the discovery of Lipitor, Viagra and Norvasc Pfizer is now a household word, and with the recent burgeoning antipathy to pharmaceutical companies, I sometimes feel as if I worked for a gun maker or producer of pornography. It was with this background that I lay in the President's room and watched the nurses bring me a pharmacopoeia of drugs. I received over 25 different drugs during my stay in the hospital including some made by Pfizer. I remember clearly coming around in the High Dependency Unit and seeing a bottle of diflucan hanging from a stand and its contents slowly dripping into my arm. Diflucan is an antifungal drug that made huge contributions to fighting fungal infections in patients with AIDS before the success of the recent protease inhibitors. A former colleague of mine, Ken Richardson, made it. He was a tall angular fellow, with a broad London accent and a smile that looked as if his dentures would explode from his mouth at any moment. He worked in Pfizer's research labs in England and loved to fish and tell jokes, especially fish jokes. Now here I was receiving his genius in a Nairobi Hospital, drip by drip.

Here is a list of all the drugs I received. As I write this, America is embroiled in the debate over the importance and value of the pharmaceutical industry. There is no doubt that this industry enjoyed decades of protection from the Darwinian forces of the market which caused other industries such as automobiles, steel and electronics to become truly competitive in the global market. Sadly, this pressure is only now being applied to the pharmaceutical industry and because of the long lead-time we are in real danger of throwing the pills out with the dirty bath water. Consider this list and the hundreds of thousands, if not millions, of people whose lives it saves and makes better, including my own.

Drug	Generic name	Function
Cordarone	Amiodorone	Cardiac arrhythmias
Clexane	Enoxaparin	Anti-clotting agent
Ativan	Lorazepam	Anxiolytic
Tazocin	Piperacillin	Antibiotic
Ciproxin	Ciprofloxacin	Antibiotic
Nimbex	Cisatracurium besylate	Neuromuscular blocker
Zovirax	Acyclovir	Anti-viral
Dormicum	Midazolam	Anxiolytic
Diflucan	Fluconazole	Anti-fungal
Stilnoct	Zolpidem	Sleep inducer
	Morphine	Analgesic
Lanoxin	digoxin	Stimulates heart contraction
Lasix	Furosemide	Diuretic
Meronem	Meropenem	Antibiotic
Coreg	Carvedilol	Anti-hypertensive
vancocin	vancomycin	Antibiotic
Klacid	clarithromycin	Antibiotic
Atrovent	ipratropium	Bronchial dilator

Losec	omeprazole	Inhibits gastric acid secretion
Solu-medrol	Methylprednisolone	Anti-inflammatory steroid
Haemaccel	Gelatin	Plasma volume expander
Mucosolvin	N-acetyl-cysteine	Reduces mucous viscosity
Avelox	Moxifloxacin	Antibiotic
Augmentin	Amoxicilin and clavulanic acid	Antibiotic

Table of medicines taken while in Nairobi Hospital

A consistent joy to me in Nairobi Hospital was the support and competence of the nursing staff I met. One nurse, Rose Maranga, would come in with my medicine and say in Kiswahili, "Hizi ndizo dawa zako." "Here are your medicines." She and all her colleagues had a reverence for the drugs that is often lost in Western hospitals. To them these drugs were precious. They treated AIDS patients every day and saw the effect of these drugs on people at death's door.

The nurses came from a variety of the over forty different tribes in Kenya, Kikuyu, Kalenjin and Luo to name but a few. They invariably had Western first names. When I asked them about this they said it was a way of everyone fitting in. One particular nurse, Joanne, was a Kalenjin, which was the same tribe as Daniel arap Moi, the former Prime Minister. Sadly, the corruption associated with him was a cloud over the heads of all Kalenjin, and she was shy about discussing her tribal origins. Conversely the new Prime Minister, Mr. Kabeki was a Kikuyu and, as a result, any Kikuyu, like Kim, the nurse who pushed me into the North Wing, was proud and optimistic about the future of Kenya. The racial tensions in Kenya are odd. There are tribal tensions but these seem to have been abated, at least in part, because Mr. Kabeki has been at pains to appoint a cabinet with representation from all tribes. There is a large Indian presence in Kenya stemming from their migration when it was a British colony. The British encouraged more than a quarter of a million to come to Kenya. The first major influx came with the building of the 950 km Uganda Railway from Mombassa on the Indian Ocean to Kisumu on Lake Victoria in 1896-1901. This is a remarkable feat filled with immense privation on the part of the Indians. The story is most famous for a pair of man-eating lions, which attacked the laborers as they built the track through Tsavo, killing 135 of them and bringing the whole enterprise to a halt for a period. These lions appeared to gain an intense liking for human flesh. Eventually Lt. Colonel Patterson, the overseer of the railway project, shot them. The lions were unusual in that they had no manes, probably because of the thick thorn in which they hunted in Tsavo, although one quaint story that does the rounds is that they had very high levels of testosterone which explained their belligerence and, as with human males, their baldness! The lions, named "Ghost" and "Darkness" were turned into trophy rugs but then purchased by the Field Museum of Chicago in 1925. You can see the lions there today where they have been stuffed and placed in a diorama, but I am afraid they look a bit moth eaten.

The descendants of these Indians quickly established themselves as efficient and profitable merchants and became a *de facto* middle class. Their children took over professional roles such as physicians and lawyers. This in turn fostered resentment amongst the native Kenya people. Two of the three doctors that treated me in Nairobi hospital were Indian, Dr. Paresh Patel, my cardiologist and Dr Gerald Moniz, the anesthesiologist who intubated me amongst other things. My pulmonologist was Dr. Muhindi. He was African and, like the other doctors, he had trained in England. Oddly, muhindi means "those from Hind or India" in Kiswahili. I did not know this then so I didn't get a chance to find out how his ancestors came by that name.

LIVING DINOSAURS

Every morning and evening at about 6 a.m. and 6 p.m. hadada ibis (*Botrytis hagedash*) would fly over the hospital. They were very comforting with their benevolent croaking *kah-a-a-a* call, and reminded me of being in the bush. Our relationship with, and influence by, these living dinosaurs is strange and I thought back to the hornbill that flew into my room in Nanyuki Hospital. I should be careful here, it is far from certain that birds are living dinosaurs or even evolved from dinosaurs. However, I do find the arguments compelling. Recently a dinosaur skeleton, *Sinosauropteryx*, was found with clear feather impressions in the rock. These impressions have been described as looking like a bird's down feathers. One theory holds that the scutes, or the thick scales seen on chicken legs and dinosaurs, have evolved from feathers. Indeed genetic manipulation has shown that blocking the action of certain proteins will cause scutes to become feathers. This raises the intriguing possibility that some dinosaur ancestors were feathered and that their later scaly covering came from feathers.

Tristan and Cindy came to see me one night when I was in the Presidential suite and were kind and sympathetic. They bought a bottle of wine. I had not touched a drop in nearly three weeks and a few mouthfuls made my head spin. After getting me a bit tipsy Tristan and Cindy took Nancy out to dinner. They went to the notorious, infamous, and now famous Muthaiga Club. Built in 1913, it was the quintessential British colonial club and tries to hang on to that faded myth to this day. The only real energy in the club comes from young white Kenyans who wrestle on the bar floor and try all sorts of puerile pranks, but it has a rather passé feel to it now. To eat in the dining room one has to sport a jacket and tie, and possess the ability to eat rather sub-standard food. I remember on one occasion I was sans both and had to resort to a dubious cloakroom filled with old jackets and ties. I selected a rather boring blue blazer but managed to set it off with the most god-awful rose moiré silk tie with white and green stripes. It came from Harrods's man's shop and I am sure is the official neckwear for the Royal Association of Ferret Buggerers. The food at the Muthaiga is execrable. However, the crazy, eccentric, faded colonial clientele and the ambience are wonderful. Tristan rode his horse into the bar on his wedding celebration. At the end of one of the long and dark corridors is a stuffed lion. Shot in the 20's it is slowly disintegrating in its glass case. Part of the disintegration is the result of Hugh Cholmondeley, the third Baron of Delemare, who used to shoot live rounds into it.

BRIT FOOD

He liked the toad-in-the-hole too, but I vetoed that. Toad-in-the-hole is venturing too far down the Brit food cesspool.

—brownbreadicecream.blogspot

The influence of the British colonial presence permeated almost every aspect of hospital life. One constant reminder of this was the food. Many things reminded me of my childhood in England in the 1950's. The tea tasted just like the tea I drank at my grandmother's when I was a small boy. Served in the same thick china cups and each time I tasted it I could see her face as she poured out the strong, orange brew. I remember passing the hospital shop in my wheel chair on the way to my daily chest X-ray and seeing Lucozade on its shelves. This was the equivalent of champagne when I was a boy. A British chemist developed it in the late 1920s as a tonic for the sick and it contained mostly glucose syrup in a carbonated water base. It was a golden fizzy drink packaged in a bottle with a yellow cellophane wrap. I think this packaging was discontinued in the 80's in England, but here it was as I remembered it during my childhood. When I was very sick with the flu, my mother would buy a bottle and I think its psychosomatic power still held sway over me, so much so that I wanted to ask the nurse to stop and buy me a bottle. My diabetes precluded me from following through on that wish. Who knows, perhaps I would have recovered much quicker had I tried it. Each day an orderly would come into my room and give me a small piece of printed-paper on which was a menu for breakfast, lunch, and dinner, and I had to select what I wanted. The menus were taken directly from those served in British schools in the 1950's leavened with the odd item one might have come across in an Indian take-away in Bradford on a cold smoky wet November night in 1963. Occasionally, just to warp your mind and remind you that you were not in fact in Bradford, they would throw in a piece of exotic fruit of the sort I had not encountered until I was about 18. Here is a typical menu with my annotations:

> *Rhubarb crumble,* surely one of England's culinary highlights.
> *Indian curry* with al dente okra
> *Consommés* that were delicious—goat especially.
> *Fresh passion fruit,* that looked like an aubergine-red dimpled pebble on which a green sea mold had grown. When I cut it open the orange green flesh fluoresced. The black crunchy seeds were sour but modulated a tone or two with sweetness—something to eat slowly, with reflection, while recuperating in Africa.
> *Khumbi banji* or ox liver hmm…let me think about that one.

At about this stage in my treatment, I stopped trying to keep control of what was happening to me. All my life I have worked hard to keep control. This is a reaction to fear. Fear of abandonment, fear of not being loved, fear of dying, just plain fear. When I reached the private room in the North Wing of the hospital, I was so exhausted that I think my brain just gave up trying to wrest control. I stopped asking questions about what was going on and if an i.v. was low I just let it run out and waited for the nurse to come rather than trying to summon her. It is hard to keep this perspective but it is a guaranteed recipe for happiness, especially, as we shall see, in riding if nowhere else. The more one tries to control the horse through conscious effort rather than feeling, the harder it is to ride and the more the horse will resist your every move. One thing my Nairobi experience taught me, less is more in things, horses, and I suspect life.

THE JOURNEY HOME

If you actually look like your passport photo, you aren't well enough to travel.

—Sir Vivian Fuchs

The day before I left I went back to the ICU to say goodbye to the people who had taken care of me. I felt so big, vital, and just plain vertical when I went into the ward. One particular nurse who had cared for me in those first days was Judy. I went up to her and grasped her lovely brown arm and hand, black skin on white, touching souls. The villages of our origins are thousands of miles and millions of words apart, so different, and yet we came from around the same ancient fireplace. Those miles and words dissolved in one touch. I hope my health gave her happiness as her kind competence gave me back my life.

Patrick met us at the entrance to the hospital and I at last got to ride in his famous taxi, the one that ferried Nancy back and forth through the Nairobi streets for over two and half weeks. He told us how he had been pulled over by a corrupt policeman just the day before and charged with an expired license. He had a perfectly good license and the cop was simply looking for a bribe. It would have been so easy for Patrick to give him the small sum he asked for but he was so incensed by the rampant corruption that he felt bound to refuse and therefore had the hassle of going to court in the sure and certain expectation that the cop would not turn up and his case would be dismissed. I admired him for that and hoped that he would succeed; we were so lucky to find such a decent man in our hour of need.

Patrick drove us to the airport and I was shuttled onto the flight in a wheel chair. We flew coach and the steward would only bring me my oxygen after he had given the first class passengers their drinks! Ha, I experienced a little frisson of rebellion. I was more sympathetic for Nancy who carried all the burden of my well-being through these petty bureaucratic trails. We stopped over in Johannesburg so I could catch my breath and arrived home some 36 hours later. My mother-in-law was at our house and when she saw me, she said to Nancy that she didn't think I would make it thought the night! And so I went from strength to strength, physical and psychological. Horses got me in but this time people got me out.

As I lay in my bed in Connecticut I was about to start a journey. This journey tested me physically, spiritually, and emotionally and as I write this, one year later to the day, I am a very different person from the man lying in Nanyuki watching a hornbill fly into his room. How did I come to be there? I now realize I was lucky, lucky to be thrust into Dante's wood at the age of 50.

Nel mezzo del cammin di nostra vita	Midway in the journey of our life
Mi retrovai per una selva oscura	I came to myself in a dark wood,
Che la diritta via era smarrita	for the straight way was lost

This is Robert and Jean Hollander's translation of the first stanza of Dante's *Inferno*. Many cite this as a metaphor for what happens to people as they move into their middle years. Suddenly people feel lost. The things that used to be important to them no longer exert their pull. The promotion, the corner office, the partner with whom they have swung through life for decades, all start to lose their salty taste and to pale on the tongue. Many get a car, a lover or a drink and emerge from this time, much as they entered it, but with a distinct loss of color and appetite for life. Others walk out one morning and do not return, and still others change within the skin of their life, like a moth emerging from a chrysalis. For these people, I like Jung's description of the middle passage as a time to wrestle with and achieve self-actualization. This is hard and brave work, and many fail. It is the time when people cease to live for parents, friends, lovers, or co-workers. Instead, perhaps though an innate realization that they have a little less time ahead of them than behind, they start to lead their own lives. If they are lucky, if they make this transition, they become their true selves. They get to live an authentic life.

I must declare myself a Darwinist and I naturally reflect to see if there is a Darwinian rationale for this process. The complement of genes we carry around with us today were pretty much done and dusted in East Africa 150,000 years ago during a time when most of us never saw the other side of thirty. Does that mean that this middle passage is just what happens to an animal with our intellectual attributes when it reaches what, 150,000 years ago would have been a very old age? Alternatively, is it a side effect of the Western capital-driven life style, wherein by the time we reach 50 many of our financial responsibilities have been eased and we are free to explore and do what we really want? Looking at other, non-Western, cultures where mortgages, expensive educations for children and progressive salary scales are not the norm may provide insight into this point. Or does this whole process reflect some sort of exhaustion of the emotional part of the brain such that it can no longer go on conditioning and programming us to live for others?

I had been thinking about my own middle passage for some time, but more from an intellectual than an emotional perspective. I read books, talked with people, and noticed changes in others and myself, but it was from a distance. Therefore, I am careful to choose the word "lucky" above to describe what happened to me in Kenya in 2004, when I found myself in Dante's metaphorical wood for real. I am sure I would not be writing this now if it were not for that event. This book tells how I came to this point and it starts in Connecticut in the autumn of 1995 with a catalog.

2

I've Killed My Husband

When a man is once run away with, the first thing that occurs to him, I imagine, is how to stop his horse; but men by no means agree in the modes of bringing this about.

—Geoffrey Gambado, An Academy for grown horsemen.

It was the autumn of 1995, I sorted the mail, casually throwing aside catalogs slick in texture and content, when suddenly one that showed three people on horseback standing in front of an elephant pulled me up short. The elephant's ears were flapping and her trunk was curled. This was no ordinary catalog. The reason it came was that a year earlier Nancy and I had been to a dude ranch in Colorado. Amidst aspens, hot tubs and east coast wannabe cowboys, we befriended a New York couple. I did not realize it then, but now come to appreciate, that this couple was representative of a very common pairing found in *homo sapiens*, specifically that of a horse-loving woman and a horse-fearing man. Most men seem to favor Ian Fleming's epigram that a horse is dangerous at both ends and uncomfortable in the middle. The man in this case was an advertising editor for the New York Times and was smart enough and confident enough to come to a dude ranch and simply choose not to ride. I, on the other hand, quite fancied myself as Clint Eastwood in *High Plains Drifter* and quickly embraced the chance to bow my legs and tan my cheeks. Over drinks around a crackling fire beneath the Colorado night we uttered that inane phrase, "we should do this more often." The "this", at least for me, was bouncing uncomfortably on top of a horse with only the ever-present grasp of fear at my throat to take my mind off the pain in my seat. Instead of simply nodding agreement to the inanity our new found friends immediately launched into a detailed description of an outfit called Equitour that organized horseback riding trips throughout the world and said they would immediately add us to Equitour's mailing list. Well, once you have been to Colorado then the world is but a small step, especially after a few Jack Daniels.

In 1995, I was not an accomplished rider (some might say that nor am I in 2005 come to that). I could not ride and when the horse I had in Colorado, rose to anything other than a trot I was not a happy man. You may ask what I was doing on a horse-riding trip given my equine limitations. The reason is that my wife, Nancy, is a rider, and a very good one to boot.

She started to ride when she was three. Now, at the age of 55, she is a skilled dressage rider. I on the other hand started to ride at the age of 42 and, well, now at the age of 51, I am not an accomplished dressage rider, but I dare say that I can trail ride. Whether this is a justified claim I will leave up to you to decide, after having sifted the evidence I am about to set forth.

I write this in the southeast corner of Connecticut at the beginning of a New England winter. The air is cold, and the leaden sky seems to suck the heat from the marrow of my bones. It is at times like these that I yearn for the plains of Africa and a horse on which to ride them. All is not gloom and doom however, for I have just returned from riding my own horse, Gideon. Gideon is a 16-year-old 17 hands 1" Dutch warmblood with a burnished copper coat and a long face. Every time Nancy sees him she says, "Why the long face Gideup?" He also has a little fatty bump between his front legs that I fondly think of as a panic button. Warmbloods, as the name suggests, originated from crosses between cold bloods such as shires and hot bloods such as Arabs or thoroughbreds. Military use drove the breeding, resulting in a horse capable of speedy attacks at the gallop, safety over cross-country terrain and agility in face-to-face combat. Alas, Gideon and I are not quite ready for face-to-face combat, but today we did make progress.

The best way to capture this progress is to say I let my weight come true with the horse. Horse riding is all about letting go, and as such is the best training for a happy life. It is hard to think of a single endeavor in which letting go will not make it better. This insight is neither novel nor profound, indeed *less is more* has become a cliché. The problem is that I know this with my left-brain but I cannot seem to get my right brain to pay attention. The result of all this is that as soon as things start to go wrong when riding, I get tense. I grip with my thighs and even my knees when things get bad, and this is an absolute no-no. Gideon immediately senses my stress and he tightens. Then we have a tight horse and a tight rider and neither of us is happy. The key to avoiding all this tightness is to relax, breathe and let your weight sink into the saddle and into your legs and down into your heels, in other words to let your weight come true with the horse. Once you have achieved this, then I think it is fair to say that you can ride.

On average, I have taken a one-hour riding lesson every two weeks for 8 years, that is 200 hours of riding lessons, to say nothing of the hundreds of hours I have spent in the saddle not being instructed. With this amount of time invested, I could be flying 747's for a Russian oil company. Instead, I can just about walk, trot and canter my horse.

A theme that you may already notice starting to emerge in this book is one of advice, advice on how to ride in Africa. The need for advice depends upon how experienced you are already. My qualification in being able to offer any advice is that at the start of these stories I had absolutely no horse sense, or at least none that proved in any way remotely useful in the African bush. However, as I spent more time in Africa I gained some hard won experience, not only from my own mistakes but also from those of my fellow travelers. Here is my most important piece of advice. If you are an aspiring rider you should master the basics of dressage, which in French means literally, training. Dressage constitutes the fundamental principles of riding and no matter whether you are going to rope cows, apply to join the Mounties or gallop across Africa it will stand you in good stead.

The origin of dressage lies in the attempt by people to train the horse for use in warfare. The invention and use of small firearms brought about the revival of dressage after its demise during the dark ages. Guns obviously presented a serious threat to mounted troops. One defense was to be able to control the horse exquisitely well and to be able to regroup them at a moments notice. While I do not often get shot at when I am riding in Connecticut, I do get challenged by all kinds of wild life when riding in Africa and the difference between a black rhino's charge and a Glock 9mm is purely academic. When these stories begin my definition of riding was the art of keeping my horse between the ground and me.

Back to the Equitour catalog, there before me were all the most beautiful and exciting places in the world, and to complement the descriptions there were photographs of people galloping through those places clearly enjoying themselves. The ride that immediately captured my attention was Kenya. I had always wanted to go to Africa but Nancy was not so keen, more through an aversion to camping than anything else. Suddenly I saw the way forward. I would learn to ride if Nancy would come with me on a horse-riding trip to Kenya. She said it was a deal, and so it began, a year of weekly riding lessons for me and then off to Nairobi. Suffice it to say I am still in one piece, and as I write this in 2005, I have been riding in Africa 11 times. I offer these short stories that try to capture my experiences in Africa. Experience in this context, is short hand, or a euphemism, for terror, excitement, stunning beauty, and life-transforming fun.

People ride in Africa for two reasons. First, they love horses and second they love adventure. When you mix horses and Africa, you get both. Adventure is really about finding the edges in your life and then putting yourself on them. These are the places where you no longer have even the fantasy of being in control of your life. When you get there, you find out a lot about whom you really are and whom the people with you really are. Sometimes that's good, and sometimes, as they say in the corporate world, you discover an opportunity for growth. Your horse is all that stands (or more frequently gallops) between you and certain death, or at least that is what you imagine. Do you know how many holes there are in Africa that are just the right size for a horse's hoof? The answer is more than the sum of photoreceptors on your and your horse's retinas and more than the number of ions that have to move in and out of both your optic nerves before you can see a hole and signal your horse not to step in it. Take this from a man who has stepped in one of two holes whilst on a horse. My first trip to Africa was a fast endurance safari across Kenya. It was one of those trips where the organizers say this is for experienced riders only, that is to say those who are comfortable galloping like bats out of hell.

When I said to Nancy that I would learn to ride if we went on a horseback safari, it sounded reasonable to all concerned. Surely learning to ride a horse at the age of 42 is easy compared with the rigors of staying in a tented camp with some 400 staff and exquisite food. I dutifully took riding lessons. Every Sunday I would go to Fox Ledge Farm in East Haddam, Connecticut, get on a school horse, and take a lesson. Fox Ledge is a dressage barn, which means the riders are serious, the horses are big, and the instructors want you to learn to ride classically. This I cheerfully did, and pretty soon I could walk, trot and canter in the indoor arena and occasionally went outside to experience a beginner's cross country, getting to practice two-point. Two-point is where you get your butt out of the saddle so that you can ride fast over uneven terrain without bouncing around on your horse's back.

When February 1996 rolled around and we set off for our first ride in Kenya, I was naïvely confident. My naiveté was compounded by the fact that I had not yet realized that the demonstrable fact that I could walk, trot and canter meant nothing because I was not doing these things correctly, my weight was not where it should be and indeed I was but a pale facsimile of a true rider.

We went to Kenya with our dear friends Astrid and Gerry. Much like Nancy, Astrid is an accomplished rider. Much like me, Gerry is not. Indeed our first experience of serious riding, was this trip. Astrid is petite with blond hair and an infectious energy and enthusiasm for life. She is also very right brained. This means that she is incapable of organizing much of anything. She is a personal dress designer. In other words, her clients come to her studio and she advises them on their couture. She is able to work with material, or should I say flesh, which is best captured in Dolly Parton's maxim of 20 pounds of mud in a ten-pound sack, and transform it into sculptured marble. Astrid is Austrian by birth but Finnish by nationality since her dad was a Finn. She has lived in Mexico and Brazil, and speaks seven languages. These include Swedish and Dutch, but of course, these are not really languages more like throat complaints. Gerry is a kaaskop (cheese head—Dutchie, as in if it ain't Dutch it ain't much), he is also a philosopher, raconteur and teller of bawdy tales. The latter can be great fun when relaxing around a campfire after a few drinks and a long day in the saddle. He is a big man with a bigger head. Indeed his head is really a sphere of Edam cheese balanced on his shoulders. At the time of the events described here, he was the Sales Director for South America for a large glue company. However, his real passion is psychology and he has since become a trained psychologist. I think this purpose was realized as we sat around many, many African camp fires.

Gerry now lives in Amsterdam enjoying the enviable life of a man who has seen and experienced the world. He lives with a woman who loves him and sees his grandchildren while living a life of modest tastes. This modesty includes forgoing alcohol and marijuana, both of which Gerry and I have been know to enjoy together. Gerry and Astrid lived in Connecticut at the time of these stories. Nancy and I saw them frequently and their friends became ours and vise versa. One especial friend was Mary, who among many exceptional talents could make the most exquisite martinis. Her recipe was to include a little vodka with the gin to "soften it." The vermouth was a suggestion. The Immaculate Conception informs the amount of vermouth one should add to a Martini. As Saint Thomas Aquinas once noted, the generative powers of the Holy Ghost pierced the virgin's hymen like a ray of sunlight through a window—leaving it unbroken.' One must find a source of light, natural is best because that means one would enjoy the martini early in the day. Make the martini without vermouth and then place a vermouth bottle between the martini glass and a ray of sunlight. The passage of light through the martini bottle is sufficient to give the right amount of vermouth flavor to the martini. I find the analogy with the Immaculate Conception to be very pleasing, and always consider that as I down my martini.

Luis Bunuel was very fond of reciting this quote and was widely acknowledged the connoisseur of the martini. Here is his recipe taken from his autobiography *My Last Sigh*. "*Another crucial recommendation is that the ice be so cold and hard that it won't melt, since nothing's worse than a watery martini. The day before your guests arrive put all the ingredients—glasses, gin, and shaker—in the refrigerator. Use a thermometer to make sure the ice is about twenty degrees below zero (centigrade). Do not take anything out until your friends arrive; then pour a few drops of Noilly Prat and half a demitasse spoon of Angostura bitters over the ice. Shake it, and then pour it out, leaving only the ice, which retains a faint taste of both. Then pour straight gin over the ice, shake it again, and serve.*" It was with the shared experience of several of Mary's martinis, plenty of *bon homie, bon vivant, bon bibine,* and the occasional puff of Mary Jane, that Gerry and I became fast friends and comrades on horse.

Nancy, Astrid, Gerry, and I laughed and drank our way across the Atlantic. We stopped in London, highly recommended when going to Africa, and stayed at the Pelham Hotel in South Kensington. That night we ate at a crazy Japanese restaurant called T'su, where the food traveled around the restaurant on conveyor belts. The food appeared on plates of different color to indicate their price and you simply swiped the food that you fancied as it passed your table. After a few Sapporos and sakes, you started swiping more plates and the gold plates always looked better than the green ones. As a result, the night slipped away in a haze of alcohol and sushi and the tab was about four hundred dollars at the end of the meal.

The next day we caught our flight to Nairobi. Astrid and Nancy were decidedly unwell as they had larium poisoning. Should you ever go to a mosquito-infested area it is wise to take something to protect against malaria, but I would strongly advise against larium, the trade name for mefloquine. Some people after taking larium have delusions, feel as if they are going to die and, unfortunately for them, generally do not. I must say Gerry and I were fine which clearly indicates that excessive alcohol is the best prophylaxis for larium poisoning. However, as with all infectious disease therapies, resistance is developing and many places in Africa contain mefloquine-resistant strains of malaria. A recent school of thought is that you should take nothing for malaria and if you get it simply take artemesin. You feel like hell for a couple of days and then you are fine. Artemsesin is an extract of artemsesia or qinghao, a plant used in China for over 2000 years to treat fevers. A couple of Chinese scientists were spared time in the Red Army in the 1970s to explore cures for malaria and came up with this extract. When used in combination with mefloquine it can cure malaria. It is readily available in Africa, wrapped in paper tubes and costing only a few dollars. It does not look very auspicious but it works.

We arrived in Nairobi at Jomo Kenyatta airport. In 1996, it was not as pleasant as it is today. As we walked through the arrivals hall all the monitors had been broken, as if someone had lobbed a brick into each one. The airport staff was very surly and there was a lot of confusion about visas and their procurement at $50 a piece. Nonetheless we were met by, our soon to become dear friend, Mark Lawrence. Mark was to be our guide on that first safari. He was born in Nairobi, after his father came over from England in 1932 as a game hunter. His dad started the Kenyan mounted police and taught Meryl Streep how to shoot for her part in the filming of *Out of Africa*. Mark started life as a jockey but couldn't keep to the weight and after a brief stint in England he joined the safari business. He has an elfin charm with curly blond hair and is a handsome fellow in both body and soul. He is also a very good guide. He is taciturn and thus not always nattering on about trivial stuff and breaking into the natural magic of the country.

Mark is very confident and competent. In addition to fluent Kiswahili, he speaks Maa, the language of the Maasai and above all, he knows horses. I remember one occasion when I was trying to cajole a couple of Maasai into letting me try out their bow. In spite of miming an arrow being drawn back and pointing vigorously at their bow I couldn't communicate what I wanted so I went to Mark and asked for some words. He gave me two, which I tried on the Maasai and *shazam* I had the bow in my hand and was receiving expert coaching on how to draw it. On refection, the words he gave me were probably the Maa equivalent of give this bozo the god dam bow and shut him up! Fooling around with a Maasai bow and arrow needs some caution as the arrow tips are painted with an extract made by boiling up the bark of the *Acokanthera schimperi,* imaginatively called the Arrow-poison tree in English, and mixing it with latex from a fig tree. A wound from an arrow tipped with this stuff leads to paralysis and death within minutes. There is no known antidote.

After squeezing our embarrassingly copious baggage into a Land Rover Mark whisked us away to Rongai. On this, our first trip to Africa, we packed the sink. After all this was Africa, who knows what you might need and what they might not have. To accommodate everything we bought two body bags the color of fluorescent blood oranges. Once packed, they were impossible to lift and thus had to be dragged through airport lounges and bounced down steps as if they contained Jimmy Hoffa. They were invariably the last bags to be loaded on the truck when we moved camp and were often the last to be brought to the tent since they required two men to handle them. A word to the wise, if you are contemplating a trip to Africa that may include a flight in anything smaller than a 747, pack what you might need for a day hike in the Appalachians, remove half of it and take what's left. For the spiritual analog of this process read Richard Leider's book "*Repacking Your Bags*" This is a great book about purpose and life and in it Richard quotes an experience when he was walking in Tanzania and had occasion to proudly display the contents of his rucksack to a Maasai accompanying the safari. After all the stuff was laid out the Maasai looked at it and said, "Does all this make you happy?"

We negotiated the traffic on the way out of the airport on the Nairobi-Mombassa road. Over the road to were metal gantries that sported a Maasai shield, the emblem of Kenya. The gantries were slowly rusting and exuding an odd mixture of tribal heritage and post-colonial decay. After leaving Nairobi, we drove 150 miles west through the Rift valley to Rongai, near Nakuru and home to Deloraine, one of the grandest examples of colonial architecture in the country. It was built in 1920 by Lord Francis Scott, a prominent early settler in Kenya.

The current occupants of Deloriane are Tristan and Cindy Voorspuy, who also own and run "Offbeat Safaris" or as some punters affectionately like to call it—Beat Off Safaris. Tristan is a character; he talks in the clipped elisions of the British upper class and is a delightful fellow full of anecdote and able to recite the *Fox's Prophecy* and Banjo Patterson's *Man from Snowy River* amongst other equine gems. He is ruddy of face probably from having been rode hard most of his life and put up in alcohol. He has a far away look to his eyes and carries his shoulders high and his body slightly twisted because of one fall too many in the bush. He was born in South Africa and educated in England where he also spent five years in the Blues and Royals. He drove a motorbike around East Africa in his youth and fell in love with Kenya where he apprenticed himself to various safaris including the inimitable Tony Church, before setting up his own show. A friend of ours was at Badminton for the horse trials and there was a stall set up by the African Horse Safari Association. She recalls Tristan wandering back to the stall with a plastic bag in which several bottles were clinking. Our friend told Tristan that such and such a person had stopped by and asked to be remembered.

"Never heard of him" said Tristan. "But he said he rode with you in Africa and spoke fondly of you." "No, never heard of him." I am quite sure he would say the same if anyone mentioned my name to him.

His wife Cindy is Kenyan and, like Tristan, a fierce polo player. She smokes like a 1930's film star and has an impish grin set off by a delightful Terry Thomas gap between her front teeth. Tristan and Cindy's life seems to hover between the developed and developing worlds. Their polo and business parachute them into a wealthy cosmopolitan world and yet their day-to-day existence is in the soul and sway of Africa.

Deloraine is on the western edge of the Rift Valley, ten minutes off the main Nakuru-Kericho road. It is set in the middle of a 5000-acre commercial farm, at 6000 ft. on the lower slopes of Londiani Mountain, a forest and bamboo shrouded volcano. The house is just what you would imagine an English Country house would look like if it were to be built using local materials in Kenya. The exterior is made of large red stone rough-cut blocks assembled by Indian masons, and vast pieces of African wood support arches and verandas. Inside the house, the mantle shelves sport skulls and ostrich eggs. The drinks' tray groans under the weight of gin and there are plenty of dogs breathing gently on the wide board floors. You feel as if you have stepped back into *Out of Africa*, or after a few gins, perhaps *White Mischief*. This atmosphere is not forced or caricatured, it just seems to flow from Tristan, Cindy, the staff, the dogs, the bats swooping through the African night to roost under the eaves of the veranda and the feint, yet ever present, scent of Africa's red dust.

Tristan's horses are mainly thoroughbreds from the Nairobi racetrack that he has converted into polo ponies and trail horses. Tristan and Cindy are fervent polo players and travel as far as India to play. In addition to the polo ponies there were some bush ponies and the occasional Boerperd. Over the years, we encountered many Boerperds on safari and came to appreciate their fine qualities. The Boerperd (and Boerperd cross), started out in Southern Africa and is an indigenous breed dating back to the 1800s and originally bred from Berban Arabs, thoroughbreds, and Javan ponies. It is an extremely hardy and sure-footed breed with much resistance against tick borne diseases. These characteristics make it such a good horse for safaris. The Boerperd name comes from their isolation in the Boer republic at the turn of the 19th century and is a fusion of the Afrikaans words for farmer and horse. Many thousands of horses died on the battlefields of the Anglo Boer War, leaving only a small number in the remote parts of the country.

Indeed many of the horses in the infamous Charge of the Light Brigade came originally from the Cape Province of South Africa. The importation of English Thoroughbreds, Hackneys, and Clydesdales to replenish the number of horses in the country, led to the creation of the Boerperd cross when they bred with the remaining Boerperds. When you are in Africa and someone claims that you are to ride a Boerperd, it is almost invariably a Boerperd cross.

On all the various trips to Africa, we have experienced a variety of mounts. All were tough, courageous and a joy to be around. I think for a horse, being on an African safari string is the ultimate selection pressure. It will quickly sort out the good from the bad and the ugly. Of all the myriad afflictions that make horses' lives tough in Africa the worst have to be the tsetse fly and African horse sickness. The name tsetse means, "fly" in Tswana and is onomatopoeic for the noise they make when flying. Tsetse flies are vectors of African trypanosomiasis, causing sleeping sickness in humans and nagana in livestock, a fatal disease of horses and cattle. The tsetse fly has colonized just under four and a quarter million square miles of Africa between 14° north and 29 ° south making it impossible to raise cattle and thus the land is largely left to the wild game.

I first encountered the tsetse fly when riding in the Okavango Delta of Botswana. We had decided to go for a mokoro ride one afternoon. The makoro is a simple dug-out canoe favored by the locals for navigating the papyrus swamp when it is flooded. As we approached the embarkation point, tsetse flies suddenly set upon us with very painful bites. It is said that only one in 10,000 flies carry trypanoso-miasis, but try telling that to me when I can't wake up in the morning. African horse sickness is a viral disease transmitted predominantly by midges. There is an inoculation but it is very rough on the horses and the other African equids such as zebra can easily spread the disease. Once infected the mortality is 75-90%. I have never been in an African stable without hearing that a horse has recently suc-cumbed to AHS.

These diseases also speak to the toughness of the owners of horse safari outfits. Africa is an unforgiving country and getting and keeping horses is hard work, especially keeping them fit enough for the rigors of a riding safari. My hat is off to them, one and all. Tristan's horses were shod only in the front and were in excel-lent condition, thriving on two hard feeds of boiled barley and oats, with alfalfa at night when on the trail.

The morning after arriving at Deloraine, Cindy took us for a ride on the farm. The ride with Cindy was a "check out the punters" ride and, sadly, I did not check out too well. The first part involves riding a narrow track with twists and turns, overhanging tree limbs, thorn bushes and some severe inclines and declines. I was fine and quite fancying myself as a rough rider until we reached open ground. Upon seeing the horizon, my horse bolted like a bat on its way out of Dante's *Inferno*. Eventually the horse ran out of wind and I managed to stop it about three miles from the rest of the group who were galloping behind me like hunters after a pack of hounds, straining to be in at the kill. As Cindy cantered up to me, she was quick to say "You'll be fine, just make a bridge with your reins." What she meant was to loop the reins back on themselves and hold them in both hands at the base of the horse's neck. However, having looked certain death in the face I really didn't register what she was talking about. *Beat Off*, I mean *Off Beat* is not a show to worry too much about the general nervousness of its punters, so the next day I was off on my first safari, but perhaps a little less confident than I was when riding around the indoor arena in Connecticut. Punters is a Brit word, defined by the Oxford English Dictionary as "A customer or client; a member of an audience or spectator; *spec.*, the client of a prostitute." The latter is really a bit tongue in cheek (as it were) and really tries to capture the essence of people who pay for dangerous thrills.

Getting to the start of the safari involved what was to become the all too familiar eight-hour drive over what Kenya laughably calls roads. The Brits built these in the fifties but ex-President Daniel arap Moi managed to ensure no maintenance was done since independence, which has resulted in some rather large potholes showing up. Some parts of the road looked like combat aircraft had strafed them. In addition to these hazards, the police are very keen on setting up roadblocks that entail hauling a barrier of vicious spikes across the road and interrogating hapless individuals until they cough up a bribe. Nevertheless, we arrived in the Loita Hills and met our horses. The Loita hills are in the south of Kenya near its border with Tanzania. They run east west and eventually roll down into the Maasai Mara. The Land Rover drove through the bush, crossing streams where we seemed invariably to get stuck. When this happened about a dozen Maasai would emerge out of nowhere. These were our first encounters with these magnificent people, wrapped in red shukas, and looking at us with intense interest. They did not mock, or laugh at us as we struggled to jack the Land Rover out of the mire. There we were, a very odd collection of pallid people all kitted out as if we were a bunch of lieutenants on leave from Monty's North Africa Desert Rats. I would have rolled on the ground had I been a Maasai. Instead, they watched us intently, the women covering their shy smiles with cupped hands. It was impossible to discern what they made of us. I often wondered why the Maasai cloaks were red. I recently read an interesting piece of analysis that was performed by evolutionary biologist Russell Hill. He studied four combat events in the 2004 Olympics in which contestants were randomly assigned either a red or a blue uniform. In 60% of the bouts, the person wearing red won, much more than would have been predicted by chance alone. The result was found only amongst men and the authors speculate that it may elevate testosterone in the wearers or decrease it in the opponents.

When we eventually arrived at our first campsite our entrance was spectacular. It had been raining and the huge yellow fever trees were dripping as we pulled to a halt. Rght in front of us, on a small rock sat a banded snake eagle, complete with a snake writhing in its talons. The eagle flew up and over us as we sat there. The camp consisted of half a dozen large traditional Aruba tents with flysheets. Inside the tents were two cots, a bedside table complete with a kerosene lamp and lion-brand matches. The ground sheet extended outside the door and there were two camp chairs and a couple of canvas bowls. The camp was simply heaven after the long drive. We stowed our gear, or rather, I should say we hauled our body bags into the tent and started to realize that it's a lot darker inside a tent than you might think. One of the net results of this is that you can't find anything. After a few days the carefully laid plans of trying to keep used from unused cloths becomes a fantasy and your whole kit becomes one big shabby mess which you roll around rather like a dung beetle rolling its ball of excrement.

We repaired to the mess tent and enjoyed a gin and tonic. I must confess right up front that no luxury was spared in terms of the provisions and this extended to dry ice to preserve a good supply of ice cubes. We sat into that first African night with a tinkling of ice in our fire-reflecting tumblers listening to the night expand around our ears.

That night we fell into a blissful sleep, listening to the insects and the water dripping off the fever trees. Then, about an hour later, we were catapulted out of our dreams by the most fearful shriek. It was not human, nor primate, nor the roar of a big animal. It may be easier to imagine the sound if you think of a cat clobbered by a closing screen door with a spring that is adjusted a shade too tight. "What was that?" asked Nancy, I had no answer and was just beginning to formulate some options, none of which involved actually going outside with my torch to investigate, when it happened again. It was directly above our tent, no more that two feet from our heads. This carried on for about an hour during which time we just accepted that it didn't belong to anything that was going to eat us. We later learned that the creator of these shrieks was a tree hyrax, which is the elephant's closest living relative and looks like a big guinea pig. Here is how the famous African naturalist, Richard Despard Estes, describes the call, "*Calls begin abruptly with a series of loud, measured cracking sounds, often compared to a huge gate with rusted hinges being forced open, followed by a series of unearthly screams, ending in descending series of expiring shrieks suggesting a soul in torment. The calls may be repeated every few minutes for periods of up to an hour.*"

We were woken the next morning with what was to become our torture and our salvation, "*Jambo, maji moto*" Kiswahili for "good morning, hot water." This softly spoken greeting was followed by the sound of water being poured into the canvas buckets and then the zip of the tent flap as one of the staff brought us coffee and Rich Tea biscuits. Each night Mark would give us a thumbnail sketch of what we might do the next day and finished his brief summary with the phrase, "So, shall we say six, seven, eight?" This meant *maji moto* at six, breakfast at seven and on the horses by eight. That sounds fine the night before but not so fine at six in the morning.

As I poked my head out of the tent that first morning I was greeted with the sight of a soft mist shrouding the horses as they stood on their long line and a Maasai in his red shuka walking behind them with his spear in hand. He was the night watchman, there to keep wild animals from attacking the horses.

Horse on a long line

Evidently, his skills in this regard have to be ranked as mixed since the previous safari had suffered a lion attack in the middle of the night at this very camp. Fortunately, one of the guests was a vet and he managed to stitch up the horses that had mostly suffered deep lacerations on their haunches.

Back at the tent, I peered into the canvas bucket. The water had the color of cocoa and came from the nearby river, after being heated in an oil drum with "a little bit of Dettol thrown in." For the non-Brits, Dettol is a strong disinfectant that turns milky white on contact with water and in my youth was usually poured down the drains in boys' lavatories at English schools. Every time I see someone add water to Pernod, I think of my *alma mater*, the City of Oxford High School for boys. It is one of the many examples of colonial British products still used in Kenya today. Another is Omo, the oddly named soap powder that I can remember my mother using every week when I was a boy.

I splashed my face with this disinfected cocoa, shaved, and joined the others for breakfast.

The horses were quietly eating their feed from bowls placed on the ground in front of them. There is much to say about these noble animals and I hope you will stay with me through these stories to learn and vicariously experience their wonderful qualities. In nearly all of our rides in Africa the horse care followed the same general routine. The horses were trucked to the start of the safari where upon arrival they were tethered to a long line strung between two trees. They seemed very comfortable with this; the tether lines were long enough for them to lie down if they wished. As we finished our breakfast, the syces tacked up our horses.

Syce is an interesting word that is widely used in East Africa and derives from the Arabic *sais* meaning one who tends a horse. The Arab verb of which *sais* is the participle charmingly comes from the Syriac *sausi* meaning to coax, and that surely says it all when it comes to horses, and people, probably. As with many Arabic words *sais* was adopted by Hindustani and then became part of the Anglo-Indian vernacular during the British raj.

The horse tack in Kenya was English. We each had a set of somewhat moth eaten green canvas saddlebags in which to carry our lunch. There is nothing quite like a sandwich which has been bounced on horseback for 5 hours at 80°F. I can strongly advise that the best filling is butter and jam; anything else looks rather like a frog that has been through a blender by the time you come to eat it.

My horse on that first safari was Top Brass. As soon as I got on and walked him, I felt as happy as a mongoose at a cobra rally. I shall talk a little later about the assigning of horses, as it is the most important part of any African horse safari. That first day, we rode out from the camp and got used to our horses and tack. We climbed hills and enjoyed the sight of black and white colobus monkeys swinging through the forests of the Loita Hills. These monkeys have long silky black and white hair and, like all monkeys, a strong desire to watch humans on horses. As we passed Maasai villages, the magic of Africa enveloped us. Specifically, the red dust with its pungent smell and taste of sweat and tin fused with the drifting smoke and the ever-present bird song. I felt my soul had returned home, I felt as if I belonged there. This was the first stirring of what was to become a strong force on me. It was a sense of belonging, something that every human yearns for. This may have been because my genome, like yours, first came together in Africa some 150,000 years ago, where the pressures of the East African countryside selected those genes.

Soon we were ready for our first serious ride. This means a ride where we leave camp, which is then struck and moved by truck some 25 miles into the future where, all being well, we will turn up later that evening.

Mark, and indeed all the other guides we have met, takes it quite easy for the first few hours as he assesses horse and rider. He tries a few trots and if no one falls off, he tries a canter. Mark had what turned out to be a rather sickening habit of prefacing every canter with an admonition to "check your saddlebags." My colleague in fear Gerry Briels, would turn to me whenever Mark said this and give me a look much as to day "Ah, well amigo, it was nice knowing you."

Before I get back to Mark's sickening habit I should tell of the time when my horse bit Gerry's whilst we were cantering. Gerry and I were riding in the Okavango Delta in 1997. We were on a game trail that meandered its way through tall orange grass. Because the grass was some 3 feet high, we had the sensation of great speed. Much like the feeling in a sports car because it is near the ground. I could have ridden that trail forever. Imagine this great pounding horse, the blue African sky, the orange grass, and the thrill of Africa. Who knew what the next bend would reveal. Eventually the trail widened, the grass disappeared, and I came alongside Gerry. All of a sudden, my horse decided to lean over and bite Gerry's horse on the neck. This was not good, for neither horse nor Gerry. There was a bit of a mêlée and Gerry hit the ground. However, Gerry was such a good-natured chap he made no complaint, he remounted and was ready to ride again.

Gerry has had some trouble from time to time, especially with rolling horses. A horse usually gives clear signals when it is about to roll. It starts to paw the ground, and then bingo, just like someone one had shot him, he disappears from under you and starts to roll. This causes a lot of consternation to rider and guide. The rider thinks he will be crushed, while the guide is much more concerned about breaking the valuable saddle. I remember a remarkable occasion; again in the Okavango, when we were standing around admiring some giraffe. They were so gentle, and their childlike inquisitive nature exuded a form of peace on all who watched them. In the midst of this revelry, there was a commotion and then blam, Gerry was on the ground, and his horse had four feet in the air, enjoying a good roll in the dust.

With this brief sketch of Gerry's riding skills, let me take you back to that the first canter in Kenya. After dutifully checking the saddlebags, we set off at a trot and then moved up into a canter. Fortunately, Mark had chosen a wide and open plain on which to try us out. Top Brass, sensing a neophyte on his back, or perhaps receiving what to him was a very clear signal from me, veered off at 90^0 to the rest of the group and moved into an extended gallop. Eventually he stopped and as Mark rode up, I received what was becoming a common but increasingly insincere refrain of "You'll be alright."

The next canter I managed to keep the horse going straight but I committed the cardinal sin of having my saddlebags slip under the horse. I could not for the life of me figure out the right knots to keep the saddle bags attached to the saddle and short of tying three grannies on top of one another I was destined to lose my bags. Gerry did not help. Every time someone said are you enjoying the ride he would say "Oh, yes, its marvelous." Then he would turn to me and stick his tongue out like that famous picture of Einstein.

Of all Mark's phrases and admonitions the one that struck most fear in Gerry and me was "*Help your horses*" by which he meant that any reasonably competent rider would be looking at the ground ahead and helping the horse to avoid holes and other hazards like black mambas, the most poisonous snakes in Africa. It was also a euphemism for "*The ground ahead is filled with bloody holes, some big enough for you and your horse, others so small you would miss them unless you were crawling on your belly but still big enough for your horse to put his leg in, trip, and send you on the road to a nasty compound fracture in the middle of the African bush with little hope of relief for half a day, possibly more.*" As if to reinforce Mark's point we rode past several aardvark holes that looked as if someone had just taken a backhoe and dug for about three hours.

To me all the exhortation to horse-help was ludicrous because all my paltry skill and concentration was focused on staying on the bloody horse and hoping that it knew what it was doing because I sure as hell didn't. My first fall in Africa occurred on the second day. We were cantering at what I would now describe as a hand gallop, fast but our hats were not streaming out behind us, which is the true indicator of speed. The sky was a cobalt blue and the ground rose to meet us. After we had been going for about ten minutes the ground began to break up and holes started to appear with increasing frequency. Mark signaled us to slow down and just as were coming into the trot Top Brass put his foot in what I would now consider a laughably small hole. However, ten years ago, it was a bloody mine-shaft and I shot over his shoulder landing on my back. As I came to, the only thought in my brain as it sloshed around my skull was "oh, please, don't let me have broken anything, please!" Fortunately, Engai the great Maasai god heard my imprecations and I was shaken but not fractured. I re-mounted, feeling decidedly sheepish.

With this brief introductory jog to riding in Africa, I can now come to the title of this tale. When we returned home I learned Nancy had said to Astrid after that first canter, "Oh no, I've killed my husband." Nancy is a horsewoman of some considerable experience and fortitude and throughout the ride she managed to retain her composure and her encouragement for my riding when, inside, she was sure that I would fall off and break my neck. I can only paraphrase Nietzsche, "What does not kill me, makes me even crazier to do it again."

I must also add that Gerry's take on all this was, "When the shit hit the fan and we entered a wild canter our women were always riding way ahead. I was invariably one of the last. I think that somehow they were always surprised to see us still around after each canter. I would love to know if a compassionate thought ever really entered their minds."

3

Riding on the Wild Side

The great advantage of a dialogue on horseback: it can be merged at any instant into a trot or a canter, and one might escape from Socrates himself in the saddle.

—George Eliot, Adam Bede

IT'S A BLACK RHINO

The black rhino is one of Africa's most magnificent animals and stories of its fierceness are legion. They have no natural predators, lions will detour around them, and a charging black rhino can disperse a herd of elephant. The only predators of this magnificent animal are humans. Apparently, we need their horns for dagger handles and impotence nostrums. Because of this, the black rhino is on the brink of extinction and its population has decreased from over a 100,000 at the turn of the 20th century to 2000 today.

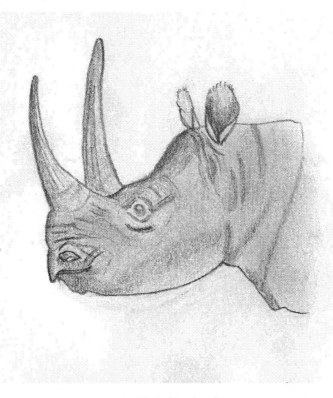

Black rhino head.

I had the opportunity of meeting a black rhino when riding in the Lapalala Wilderness of South Africa. Lapalala is a 20,000-acre reserve bordered by the Palala and Limpopo Rivers some 330 km north of Johannesburg. Our guide on this trip was Wendy. She has close set brilliant, hard eyes and a sexy South African toughness, rather like that I imagine the American cowgirls of the 1850s possessed. She often bemoaned the absence of men in the Lapalala wilderness and would recount her experiences as she went on horse trips to other parts of the world. I remember her vividly describing her trip to Argentina where she rode with a band of fearless and handsome gauchos. Sadly all but one were married and as they drank around the fire each night one by one these Latino gods would disappear leaving the only single gaucho who had squiffy eyes and a very strange personality. She treats men and women equally, truly enjoys people, and has a great sense of humor. She does not take herself too seriously; the safaris are fun for her. She does like things her own way but is respectful of her horses without being hysterical, a condition which some horse safari guides have exhibited in large measure.

In addition to Wendy, we were the usual odd bag of punters: Astrid, Ian, and Nancy from the U.S. Jürgen, Friedrun, Denis and Mary Ann from South Africa and Jez, a freelance journalist from England.

Jürgen was born in the Great Karoo of South Africa and grew up in a traditional Afrikaner family following his father's move to South Africa to escape Hitler. He is the kindest of men and one from whom I have learned much about Africa, horses, and life. He had two uncles, one died on the Eastern Front but the other, Ernst, is an intellectual and was chosen by Werner von Braun to work on the V-1 and -2 rockets. As the war ended, the German rocketeers holed up in an abandoned fortress in the Alps and sent out von Braun's younger brother on a bicycle to surrender to the Americans. The latter quickly realized the strategic importance of these people and shipped them off the States along with parts of the V rockets and all their papers. This group eventually ended up in an abandoned military base in Huntsville, Alabama. When the USSR beat the USA into space with the launch of Sputnik, Kennedy had letters sent out to various people to ask for suggestions as to how to regain America's prestige. Von Braun received one of these letters and, along with the other expatriate German rocketeers, suggested that America could probably beat the USSR to a manned landing on the moon.

The other uncle, who died on the East Front, disappeared at Stalingrad, which is still the most costly battle in human history in terms of casualties, 1.1 million Soviet soldiers and 100,000 civilians and 500,000 German and axis soldiers in a period of eight months from June 1942 to February 1943. As is so often the case all of it was due to the ferocious egos of two leaders, Hitler and Stalin. Hitler determined to take Stalingrad for many reasons but foremost was the psychological effect he thought he could achieve in capturing a city named for his enemy. Stalin was acutely conscious of this. When there are such emotional underpinnings to a battle, and when two such desperate psychopaths hold them, the resulting human misery is profound. Yet, there is another story here and that is the difficultly in winning an urban war against an indigenous army fighting house to house and, in the case of Stalingrad, room to room. The Germans bitterly joked about having captured the kitchen but still fighting for the living room.

Jürgen's wife, Friedrun or Schatzi, as Jürgen likes to call her, is the most delightfully energetic person I have met. She is slight with a taught, muscular body and blond hair. She is German and has a sharp edge of decisiveness that is wonderful to encounter and a challenge with which to joust. She does astonishing impressions of aristocratic Brits that come off sounding like a cross between the Muppets and the Duke of Edinburgh.

She owns a leopard tortoise named Goliath who spends most of his time out at stud when he's not crawling around their jewel-like garden overlooked by Table Mountain in Cape Town. Over the years, both Jürgen and Friedrun have become our fast friends. Fast as in tight and fast as in galloping on horses in the African bush.

Jürgen and Ian in Damaraland

The other couple we met on the Lapalala trip, Dennis and Mary Ann, currently live in Cape Town but spent most of their lives in the Congo, where they raised their family, leaving only after squads of revolutionary soldiers had swarmed thorough their house for the tenth time. Mary Ann tells fascinating stories of their life in the Congo. They were, and still are, keen horse riders. There life is succinctly captured by the fact that they had a parrot in the Congo who was very fond of women, especially blondes. However, his fondness did not extend to Denis whose toes he liked to bite.

As these brief character sketches suggest, we were a very affable group as we rode through Lapalala, cantering alongside red hartebeest that had the delightful trait of springing up on all fours when they were excited. You can imagine us riding along at a good clip and these beautiful creatures bounding in to the air and running along beside us. We also came within 10 yards of white rhino and generally lived the African experience.

Which rein is reverse?

I should say in passing that white rhino are huge, especially when seen from horseback, however they are docile and have very poor eyesight and unless you really threaten them or their calves, they are relatively safe. Not so black rhinos. The main difference between white and black is that the former are grazers and have a square mouth for chomping the grass efficiently. Black rhinos have a pointed mouth with prehensile lips for pulling leaves off bushes. In addition, black rhino are very aggressive. As we rode through Lapalala Wendy did a brilliant job in telling us stories about black rhino that gradually transformed these magnificent animals into demi-gods. She told us stories of how people had been caught by black rhino. Typically, black rhino are very shy, browse in the bush, and are thus difficult to see. As a result, people dismount and all of a sudden, they have a black rhino in their life. As you might imagine the rhino like to insert their horns where the sun doesn't shine and toss you in the air. Wendy told the story of the head of the Lapalala reserve as he was tracking a female black rhino. The first thing he knew she charged at him out of the bush. There were no trees around so he vaulted over a game fence cutting himself badly on the wire. The rhino bounced off the game fence and then knocked it down. The warden scrambled up a bush and the rhino proceeded to lift him out of the bush and toss him in the air four times. The last time she gouged a hole in his calf. As she was getting ready to kill him, he kicked her on the top lip and she ran away. The moral of this story is that should you find yourself *in extremis* with a black rhino, the key to life and future happiness is to kick the rhino on its top lip. Apparently, they do not like this and will bugger off.

I cannot tell you how many stories I have heard in my travels through Africa of how to extricate myself from the clutches on wild animals by simply keeping cool and doing some odd thing. I have just told you what to do if tossed by a black rhino. For every wild animal, there seem to be tried and true counsels. For example, crocodiles do not like to get their eyes poked; lions do not like you to stand still and so on. Every time I hear one of these sage pieces of advice I respectfully nod my head and privately think, you have to be kidding! I imagine myself dragged into a river by a crocodile and remembering to poke it in the eye. Not running away from a lion is almost a common place. I remember PJ, our guide in the Okavango Delta, telling me that he was once leading a group of Finns through the bush when a lion charged them. He shouted the lion down once, but it charged again, at which point he let off a round from his gun. Incredibly, the lion charged a third time at which point PJ let off another round and the lion retreated. As PJ turned around to check on the Finns, they were nowhere to be seen. To a person they had all shinned up trees as if they were a troop of baboons.

The rhino stories, apocryphal or not, were a very good incentive to stay on our horses come what may. Therefore, we rode around always listening and looking for the now thoroughly talked up fire-eating, anus-spearing animals that could easily become one's nemesis incarnate. We rode by a rhino boma. This consisted of huge tree trunks set into the ground and bolted together with steel plates. It looked like something out of Jurassic Park for retaining a stegosaurus. It was a halfway house used to contain rhinos that were being introduced into the Lapalala wilderness from elsewhere. Every hour we filled in a little more background about the black rhino, such that the envelope of our imaginations seemed to encompass a myriad fearsome attributes and the black rhino was fast becoming an almost mythical beast.

We had been riding for 5 days; the weather was perfect, the sky a clear robin's egg blue, and temperatures were in the low 80s. Periodically we would cross the Palala River, cobalt blue as it bubbled over rocks, and then we would plunge into the bush on narrow game trails. The forgoing is the verbal equivalent of a movie scene in which the happy couple is walking along a path in a sun-drenched wood. It is only the eerily swelling music that warns the audience that the woman's serial axe-murderer of a first husband is lurking behind the next tree. As we were walking along a narrow game trail, we broke one of the cardinal rules of horse-back safaris, one that incidentally gets broken all the time and usually on the first day. When I say broke, I should say that we never obeyed it, however we flaunted it on this day. Specifically we fell into lively conversation with our riding partners, telling jokes, laughing, and generally feeling good. It was in this state that we rounded a curve in the track and came upon, you guessed it—a black rhino! Wendy immediately cried out to turn and get the hell out of there. Well, that's fine but we were on a narrow track and there was not a great demonstration of manners or chivalry. Imagine half a dozen horses and riders springing 10 feet in the air and, like the mouse in a Tom and Jerry cartoon, turning 180° in mid-air. As we hit the ground, we moved from stationary to 150 m.p.h and took off like a bunch of punters being chased by a black rhino in the Lapalala Wilderness. There was an awful lot of shouting behind us and we were all convinced that our new-found friends were being tossed in the air like pizza dough and we didn't want to think what was happening when they landed. We zoomed ahead, ducking the low hanging branches and galloping along the narrow trail as if we were just out of the starting gates at Pimlico. Well, as it turned out, the rhino gave up after a couple of hundred meters and all the shouting came from Wendy trying to get us to stop galloping. She was naturally afraid that we would fall off or get clobbered by a branch. About 2 km later, we all stopped and looked back as Wendy came galloping towards us. She was not pleased—but we were—we had seen a black rhino and still had the right number of holes in our bodies!

The Lapalala Wilderness is huge and beautiful and gives the impression of natural wilderness, but it is fenced. The only place left on earth where you may get the chance to see an unfenced black rhino is Damaraland in North West Namibia, and it was with the distant hope of seeing one that we embarked on a riding safari along the Ugab and Huab riverbeds of Damaraland.

SABINE AND THE ORYX

*Again the early-morning sun was generous with its warmth. All the sounds
dear to a horseman were around me—the snort of the horses as they cleared
their throats, the gentle swish of their tails, the tinkle of the irons as we flung
the saddles over their backs—little sounds of no importance, but they stay in
the unconscious library of the memory.*

—Thomas Wynfors Vaughan

Damaraland is in the north west of Namibia, a land remarkable for its dramatic
landscapes; Jon Manchip White called his book on Namibia "*The Land God
Made in Anger.*" Damaraland is a dry, desert place inhabited by about 100 000
Damara and a few ranchers of colonial German decent. The Damara used to
occupy much of central Namibia but persecution by colonials and other tribal
groups such as the Herero and the Nama, with whom they share a common language, have pushed them into this desolate north western enclave. The western
border of Damaraland is the Skeleton Coast, so called not for imagined bones
bleaching under the African sun but for the hulks of ships that have run aground.
These wrecks are scattered all along the 400 or so kilometers of the coast, the
result of an almost constant south-westerly oceanic wind that blew them on shore
and gave the coast its macabre name. I once flew up the Skeleton Coast and could
still see the rusting hulls, marooned in seas of sand. The wind blowing over the
sand created a petrified silica sea on which these wrecks sailed, their bows plowing
through the sandy foam. The marooning sand blows in from the Kalahari Desert
in the west. The South Atlantic off the Skeleton Coast is home to the Benguela
current that conveys water from the freezing Antarctic Ocean up to the Bight of
Benin. The same wind that wrecked the ships, cooled off by the Benguela current, pushes under the warm inland air masses as they blow over the desert from
the Kalahari. This causes air inversion, which in turn prevents any turbulence or
rain clouds from forming. As a result only 10mm of rain falls per year in the land
along the Skeleton Coast. This meteorological phenomenon has produced the
oldest desert on earth—the Namib. Namib means "nothingness" in the San language. San being the name Bushmen use to describe themselves and comes from
the Nama word meaning "to inhabit."

This ancient desert probably has not changed much since the Benguela current
started some 5 million years ago. The Namib is fascinating for its flora and fauna;

indeed its whole ecology has evolved to enable it to survive on the low rainfall. The most important form of moisture is fog, formed as the warm oceanic air cools as it blows over the Benguela Current. Beetles stand on their heads, condense the water in the fog on their carapaces, and let it run into their mouths. Plants secrete salt on their leaves to take up the moisture from the fog and the remarkable *Welwitschia mirabilis* is able to absorb moisture directly from fog. This plant, found only in northern Namibia, has two leaves and lives to be several thousand years old. These leaves fray over the years and are chewed on by the occasional black rhino desperate for the, albeit bitter, moisture to be found in them. It is an otherworldly experience to come across these ancient plants and imagine them battered by wind and sand storms for more than a millennium.

Welwitschia mirabilis

It was into this place that we rode in the spring of 2003. Our small party consisted of two French people, Sabine and Bernard, a Dane, Melina, my South African friend Jürgen and yours truly. Jürgen and I had ridden together with our wives in Kenya and South Africa and this was a chance for the two of us to go it alone in the wilds of Damaraland. In addition to the punters, there was the guide, Waldi, who owned and ran the safari with her husband Lumpi and two of her friends, Hanneliese and Detlev. Hanneliese took care of the horses and administered life saving back massages around the campfire. Each morning she and Jür-gen would conduct a "Grand Rounds." They would go down the line of horses, checking them and administering patent nostrums; Vaseline and comfrey for rope burns, tea-tree oil and honey for all minor cuts. I would take my first cup of coffee from the pot sitting on the coals and watch, from a distance, this gentle, purposeful ministration to the horses. Detlev was a southwest farmer. He looked like a harness that had been too long in the sun. However, the hero of this story is Sabine.

Sabine is beautiful in that Simone de Beauvoir French way. Some 77 years old with a face filled with character and experience. Eleanor Roosevelt said "Beautiful young people are the accidents of nature; beautiful old people are works of art." Bernard, her companion and friend, was an engineer who had worked on Con-corde. He spoke little English, which, much to his amusement, gave me a great opportunity to practice my pidgin French. He took great delight in teaching me a little French song that he would croon whilst grooming his horse:

C'est si bon de siffler un whisky,
Avec une chouette souris,
Telle qu'la môme vert de gris

C'est si bon de partir n'importe où,
Bras dessus, bras dessous,
En chantant des chansons.

C'est si bon, de se dire des mots doux,
Des petits riens du tout,
Pendant que nous dansons

C'est si bon!

I find this virtually impossible to translate, however the sense is one of drinking whisky with a pretty girl, and walking arm in arm, whispering sweet nothings and dancing, well at least I think it is!

We trucked our horses up from Windhoek, the capital of Namibia, to Twyfel-fontein. This is the site of some of the most well preserved San rock carvings in existence. Estimates date the carvings to be 6000 years old and depict, amongst other things, seals. This is most interesting because in order to have seen seals the Bushmen would have had to travel the 125 km from Twyfelfontein to the Skeleton Coast and back. In addition, there were carvings of an ostrich with four heads that could have indicated that it was drinking—a San artist's attempt to pre-empt Edward Muybridge. Other carvings show the elevation of an animal in silhouette and yet its feet are shown in plan, perhaps to instruct young San hunters what the animal's tracks looked like.

Our journey followed the dry beds of the Huab and Ugab Rivers. These rivers are ancient systems dating from the Carboniferous, 300 million years ago. Most of the time, they are dry, but occasionally they will flood when rain forms inland. They last flowed continuously some 2 million years ago when they cut 100-meter gorges into the desert, exposing rock strata that snake up and down in wildly contrasting colors. In spite of being so ephemeral and only flowing above ground for a few days each year, these rivers are ecologically vital in this parched land. The subterranean waters underlying the rivers are shallow enough in places to fill hollows and sustain a wildlife population that includes the rare desert elephant. There is much debate as to whether these elephant constitute a subspecies of the African elephant, *Loxodonta africana africana*. They are smaller and have bigger feet, which, teleologically, might suggest an adaptation to living in the desert. However, the data suggest that desert elephants are actually savannah elephants that have adapted to the rugged lifestyle of the barren desert. On the other hand, researchers have determined that the smaller elephants found in forests, typically of the Congo, are indeed a distinct subspecies, *Loxodonta africana cyclotis*, from their savannah cousins of East Africa.

Rainfall in Damaraland is typically five millimeters per year. Incredibly, significant rain had fallen a few weeks before our arrival for the first time in ten years. This produced an awe-inspiring bloom of flowers and grasses sprung from seeds that must have lain dormant for more than a decade. I remember riding out on an early day in the safari with tall green grass brushing against my horse, Metallic's belly. Because of the rain, we had the chance to see many rare plants in flower. For example, we came across *Lithops ruschiorum*. This looks like a small pebble, perhaps an inch across with a delicate pink-gray skin and dimpled veins. When we saw it, pink flowers were coming out as if they had split the pebbles in half.

We left the rock carvings at Twyfelfontein and entered the valley of the Huab. The sides of the valley towered over us with ferocious rocks bristling with jagged edges. The strata of the ravaged earth showed through in seams of minerals, which curved up and down, like a writhing snake.

As we rode down the valley we could see pools of what looked like frozen water, but as we came upon them, the ice revealed itself to be salt. I dismounted and when I stepped down, the salt crust crunched and dissolved into the brackish water beneath it. The baking sun evaporated the water to leave minerals looking like a painter's palette of primrose, amber, ochre, and burnt sienna.

We had been riding for many hours when the valley became even narrower and the sides almost seemed to close over us. As we rounded a bend, we could see a house in the distance. This was a rhino tracker's station and home to Bernd, his wife and two year old daughter. The horses could smell water and began to become excited, or at least that is what we thought. We rode into an opening in the valley containing sand and a few reeds that were able to tap into the subterranean water. We dismounted and Waldi told us to water our horses at the water hole rather than having to haul buckets up to the long line. We led our horses down to the pool when suddenly all hell broke loose. Horses were rearing and plunging, people were in danger of being squashed, it was a mess, and it was all because a herd of elephant had come though the previous day and drunk from the water. It was the aroma of elephant that had excited our horses and not the prospect of water. No amount of cajoling would get the horses into the water, much less drink. Bernd the rhino tracker went into the pool and tried to pull in a horse, the horse pulled him out. After a while, it began to look like a point of honor and Jürgen and I wanted to just go and have a beer rather than be trampled by our own mounts. Adding extra spice to this mêlée was Bernd's Alsatian dog, which was running in and out between the horses' legs with a huge rock in its mouth and managing to bark in the most impressive manner. I think this was the first canine ventriloquist that I had ever met. I am sure he could also bark whilst drinking. Fortunately after 30' of this, the guides threw in the towel and proceeded to cart water in buckets as per usual. As Dorothy Parker famously although somewhat unfairly said, "You can lead a whore to culture but you can't make her think." A weak paraphrase might run: "You can lead a horse to water but it better not have elephant stink."

Bernd's rhino tracking station is remote, 150 kilometers to the nearest town. Each day he goes out and looks for rhino, photographs them, and provides data to the Save the Rhino Trust. It was poignant that after I left his camp and returned home to the U.S. I learned that at the very time we were with him a Dutch couple was dying of thirst less than 5 km from the camp. They had been driving a 4X4 and their vehicle broke down. Not knowing there were any people nearby they stayed with the vehicle and the man died of thirst. His wife was delirious when Bernd found them after they had been stranded for 5 days.

After we left Bernd's house we crossed several open plains as we headed south to pick up the Ugab River valley. As we rode across the plains, we came upon a rhino rubbing rock. This rock must have looked ideal to some ancestral rhino, because countless generations of black rhino have followed his lead to remove the irritation of Kipling's breadcrumbs. As a result, the rock was worn smooth and had a wonderful oily reek to it. Alas, we saw no black rhino on this trip but the very land seemed to exude their presence.

We approached the Ugab Valley surrounded by acres of brilliant yellow flowers that had exploded in the last few days due to the rains. It was like entering a sunlit meadow after the furnace of the Huab Valley. In addition to this beautiful floral benefit from the rain, we also encountered a more dangerous consequence. We rode in and out of beds of reeds, following small game trails in the beautiful yellow sand. All of a sudden, Metallic's foot sank below the hoof and he came to a halt, then the other hoof started to sink and he pushed himself back. We had run into quick sand. We quickly elected to ride on the sides of the gorge rather than risk the quick sand. I remember thinking at the time of my dad putting his hands over my eyes when we were watching some film on our black and white television in which a man was about to disappear under quick sand. I must have been about five and my dad determined that it was not suitable for my tender eyes. Of course, the net result of this was for me to imagine all kinds of horrors associated with death by quick sand. Fortunately, I did not tell Metallic about them. The riverbed was wide, perhaps 100m across, dotted with grasses, shrubs, and dry water channels. The sides of the riverbed rose at a 60° angle for some 80-90 m. Much like the Huab, the geological strata laid bare by the ancient erosion show convoluted layers of black and white rock.

We were enjoying our ride and the spectacle of a magnificent kudu, complete with spiral horns, which ran up the rocky side of the valley and stopped majestically at the top to gaze at us imperiously before disappearing over the rim.

I must digress for a moment to talk of Waldi and Lumpi, formally know as Waltraut and Albert. They are a couple that lives on a farm outside Windhoek in Namibia. I never really understood how they came by these nicknames however I believe that they are common names for Dachshunds in Germany. Personally I can see no resemblance and I should know as Nancy and I are the proud owners of a dachshund, who happens to be called Waldi, I mean Sadie. Lumpi wears what looks to be a German Panzer corporal's cap nearly all the time and I have never seen him in anything other than shorts and boots. He has a bushy beard and a kind and wise face. He is fond of putting his hand over his face and eyes when asked an asinine question by some effete punter. Waldi seems perennially young and her pale skin and blond hair belie the hours she has spent riding through the dry, scorching deserts of Namibia. From time to time she wears a bandana over her face and appears to the world as a tough bank robber. Lumpi and Waldi are of German origin, indeed Lumpi's great-grandfather was a Shutz-truppe who, along with his horse, jumped into the South Atlantic, swam ashore and found a route from what is now Swakopmond to Windhoek along the bed of the Swakop River. The Namibians invited the Germans in at the end of the 19th century as a way of holding back the trekboers who were moving in from South Africa. The trekboers were the original Dutch immigrants into the Transvaal, but the word came to be used for pioneers in general. The Shutztruppe formed the basis of this protection, but as in so much of colonial history, they came to dominate the Namibians. Lumpi found his great grandfather's notes of these exploits and decided to recreate the trip in the reverse direction. In so doing, he and Waldi started one of the toughest rides in the world. It begins on their farm, Hilton, some 25 miles outside Windhoek and then proceeds across the Namib Desert finally following the dry riverbed of the Swakop River to the South Atlantic Ocean. Upon arriving at the sea, Lumpi and Waldi give you the most delicious sandwiches and champagne and you get to try to convince your horse to swim in the sea. As you may remember, the Benguela current conveys water up from the Antarctic Ocean and you will have some appreciation as to why few, if any, horses are dumb enough to comply with this request. One of the many exciting experiences on the Namib Desert ride are the fast gallops that Lumpi is so fond of staging. On some open plain, he would line up the horses, I can still hear the jingle of the bridles as we waited. I remember thinking that this must be what the start of the Charge of the Light Brigade sounded like. Then, all of a sudden we were off, galloping like hell to some ill-defined goal. The desert is sand embedded with gravel. It is the perfect footing and I can say that I have never ridden faster, nor with more peace of mind, than on those famous Namib gallops.

I cannot leave Lumpi or the Namib without talking about the end of the Namib ride. We had been in the desert for 12 days, experiencing dust, speed, and German culture. The day before we reached Swakopmond, we camped in the dry Swakopmond River bed. By this time, my inestimable friend Gerry had had enough of riding and had elected to travel in the truck between camps. I think I know what caused him to throw in the reins as it were. We were camped in the desert and, being the desert, there was little or no bush. In the morning Gerry had to relieve himself, which necessitated him hiking about three hundred yards in his underpants with an entrenching tool over his shoulder to find a very small bush that could afford him some modestly. The look on his face as he returned from the expedition was memorable.

Gerry, before coming on these rides with us, liked to vacation in luxury inns on the Baja Coast of Mexico where he would lie under the sun drinking caipirinhas, a drink he first tried when he and Astrid lived in Brazil. It is made from the pulp of crushed limes and sugarcane liquor called chachaca. I freely admit I may have sampled one or two glasses of this ambrosia at their house. It is interesting to note that it is now the *in* drink in New York and London. Oddly, or perhaps to keep its edge, Rio de Janeiro now amuses its club patrons with caipirinhas made with sake instead of chachaca.

Because Gerry was now bouncing around in the provision truck rather than on the back of a horse, he was at the campsite ahead of us. Gerry, being a noble creature, had set up the sleeping cots and spread the sleeping bags on them so that when Astrid arrived she would not have to bother with these chores.

As expected Astrid was overjoyed to see everything set up, alas the trees under which Gerry had chosen to put the cots were infested with ticks which were happily dropping on the sleeping bags. After much shrieking and swearing, Astrid and Gerry eventually managed to shake the ticks out of their luggage and we ate supper and retired for the night.

The next day we rode into Swakopmond and enjoyed the previously mentioned champagne and sandwiches. Then came the sting in the tail. We were booked into a rather unusual hotel. It consisted of cinder block chalets painted sky blue and surrounded by electrified barbed wire on which were metal signs featuring skulls and crossbones and the word "Achtung!" in short it was Stalagluft 3. The walls were bare; it was cheap and very nasty. This was the final straw for our German tolerance. I completely lost it and became hysterical, goose-stepping around the room whilst doing an impersonation of John Cleese doing an impersonation of Basil Fawlty doing an impersonation of Goebbels. When Nancy had stopped crying and laughing and controlled me, Astrid burst out of their room saying "no way." This exclamation was in response to what I thought was the very reasonable request made by Gerry that she remove a tick, which had attached itself to Gerry's testicles. How do you define friendship? It has been said by an authority that no greater love hath one man for his brother than that he lay down his life for him. I think right up there with this is that no greater love hath one man for his friend that that he pick ticks off his balls. I did the job with aplomb. It was at this time that we decided to effect the great escape from Stalagluft 3 and we made a break for the center of Swakopmond intent on finding some decent food. We ended up at the Hansa Hotel, voted the best hotel in Namibia in 1996/7. This was a plush place with foyer, reading room, bar, dining room and reception rooms in which civilized people talked in small groups whilst drinking cocktails. We sat down and ordered champagne and Walwisch bay oysters. We enjoyed this enormously, laughing, drinking, and contrasting it with Stalagluft 3. To top off our Swakop experience, we returned to find that Lumpi was cooking us dinner in his little cell within the camp. We all turned up to enjoy some slimy white fish and slimy rice cooked in the muddy little court yard of his cell block—memorable.

To return to our ride in the Huab River bed, there we were chatting and gazing around as our horses walked along a narrow game trail in the rocks avoiding the quick sand in the riverbed. Unfortunately, Sabine did not see the tree branch that reached out over the path in front of her. She was knocked to the ground, hitting her head on a stone. We gathered around, anxiously shading her prone body from the already fierce sun. At last, she came to and was able to sit up and eventually get back on her horse. We were about 20 km from our next camp and there was only one way to go—forward into the Huab.

Forward into the Huab

We set off following fresh hyena tracks in the moist sand and watching a martial eagle soar over our heads. By noon, it became clear that Sabine was not doing well. We stopped under a huge camel thorn tree to give her some water and consider our options.

After some consultation, Hanneliese and Detlev decided that we had to press on for another 5 km at which point the riverbed would be clear enough so that we could send a Land Rover back from our next camp to pick up Sabine.

We reached the clearing and found a cave in the side of the valley that provided shelter from the sun. Jürgen and Hanneliese stayed with Sabine while the rest of us rode with the loose horses to camp. We set off cantering and galloping for 15km along the winding riverbed. The loose horses ran in between us kicking and bucking, the sun was starting to set and we had that thrill and urgency of an adventure to be savored and a mission to accomplish. As we turned one bend in the riverbed, we came upon a lone oryx. He was a beautiful bull with striking black and white stripes over his lustrous taupe coat and a pair of magnificently curved horns. Four people galloping together with three loose horses were not what he expected, or wanted, to see so he took off and for about 3 km, we cantered with him. The graceful lope of the oryx, magnified by his horns and the drumming of our hoof beats on the sand as we wound through the narrow valley of the Huab was thrilling. Eventually Bernard's horse began to tire and he had to change mounts. We stopped, switched saddles and off we set again. You can imagine the expression of the oryx's face as we came around the corner again. He had probably never seen a horse before much less seven, twice within the hour and coming straight for him at a full gallop. He decided that enough was enough and he took off up the side of the valley, pausing at the crest to look back on us to make sure he had not imagined all this, before he disappeared.

Oryx

We arrived in camp and dispatched the Land Rover, which brought Sabine safely back to camp. Sabine was in fine form the next day, although a little stiff and we headed off towards the Skeleton Coast. Many days later when we reached the sea at the southerly end of the Skeleton Coast, we made our last campfire on the beach. The wind was blowing and we could smell a dead seal or two rotting on the shore and now providing dinner for the jackals that trot up and down the beach.

On that final evening as we sat around the campfire talking about our trip we spontaneously stood up and sang, "For she's a jolly good fellow" to Sabine, a woman whom I will never forget. Here is a picture of Sabine with her friend's pet cheetah in Paris some years ago.

Sabine

RIDE OF THE LONG NECKS

As we came across a plain in the Loita Hills of Kenya, we could see the necks in the distance. We came closer and closer and more and more of the necks came up to look at us. The benevolent, inquisitive look combines with long brown eyelashes and a lolling tongue to confer a sense of childlike wonder on giraffes. We stopped about 50 yards away from them and sat on our horses. We were on a flat golden plain dotted with deep green acacia trees. The branches of acacia form layers of flat green surfaces and give the East African savannah its characteristic appearance as well as providing the most perfect of perches for Africa's many birds of prey.

It is important to remember that if you intend to ride in Africa fearsome thorns arm almost every plant you will encounter. The net result of which is that your fancy designer safari shirt is quickly shredded in spite of what it says in the catalog about how it was developed in East Africa by macho white hunters and has been tested in the toughest bush. All of this is absolute bullshit intended only to convince weekend yuppies to buy their stuff. Take, for example, the whistling thorn (*acacia drepomalobium*), of which there are about 18 billion acres in East Africa. Each thorn is an inch long and most have a gall at their root in which live a species of ant, which secretes a fiery substance. This interesting little set up is a classic example of symbiosis. When animals start to browse on the thorn, or rider's legs brush against them, the ants come out of the gall and do their number, the animals retreat and ant and bush are happy. Old thorns which have been vacated by the ants make a whistling sound as wind blows across the entrance hole. Wait-a-bit thorn, as the name might suggest, has wicked crescent shaped thorns that snag the smoothest of surfaces and keep you pinned down as you struggle to free your riding breeches from their sickle grasp.

The horses started to eat grass and a peacefulness descended on us, made even more pleasant by the silent gaze of the giraffe. Mark suggested that if we ride slowly towards the giraffe they would canter with us. We started to trot at which point the giraffes started walking. A giraffe's walk is faster than your average bush pony's trot, so we moved up into a canter at which point the giraffes started to lope. They hardly seemed to be stirring as judged by the speed at which their legs moved, and yet they were outpacing the cantering horses and mesmerizing me with their undulating necks. This also explains the origins of the word "giraffe" which comes from the Arab word *zarafah,* which means "the one that walks very fast." Interestingly the scientific name for a giraffe is *Camelopardalis* which derives from the Latin for camel (*camelus*), and leopard (*pardus*) because years ago it was thought that giraffes were part camel and part leopard.

It is fascinating to watch giraffe move because, together with camels, they walk right front foot, right hind foot, left front foot, left hind foot, rather than right front foot left hind foot. I am at a loss to come up with an explanation for this, I can't think of a survival advantage, and if there is one, why haven't more animals co-evolved this particular method of moving. I can't see any immediate and unique link between camels and giraffe.

We must have ridden with the giraffe for about ten minutes during which time they would never go in a straight line. Every three stride they would veer off at

90° for another three strides. After having some fun with us, they decided that they had had enough and broke off into the denser bush. As our group came together, everyone was talking about the wonderful experience. To get a sense of what it was like for Gerry and me I think Gerry summed it up by saying that all he saw were giraffe hooves from under his horse's neck as he was hanging on for dear life.

Speaking of necks, a giraffe's neck contains the same number of vertebrae as a human neck, seven; it's just that they just happen to be bigger. I have a giraffe vertebra that I found in a curio shop in Arusha, Tanzania. I remember well going into the shop. At first, it seemed very unpromising, filled with new bric-a-brac. But true to fantasy, and perhaps form, there were several boxes of old stuff. As I rummaged through many dusty Maasai bracelets, I came across some beautiful elephant and giraffe vertebrae, which Maasai had carved and dyed with mud and tobacco juice. The author, Gillies Turle was the first to recognize these artifacts for what they were, sculpture by Maasai who prior to Turle's findings in the late 80's were thought to lack any artistic culture beyond their beaded jewelry. Turle published a book called "The Art of the Maasai" showing his discoveries complete with photographs by Peter Beard. They remind me of sculpture by Henry Moore. For a few dollars, I am now the lucky owner of some of these beautiful things. My giraffe vertebra is carved into a pestle. It stands on the pointed bones and the saucer shaped place where the vertebral cartilage normally resides acts as mortar. East African medicine men or mundunugu, crush, and powder leaves and herbs in pestle and mortars just like this.

Giraffes (*Giraffa camelopardalis*) have been and still are a great crutch for creationists who claim that a giraffe could not have evolved. Their argument rests on the observations that a giraffe needs a large heart (24 lbs) to pump blood all the way to its head. The vessels in the neck contain a series of special one-way valves to regulate blood flow, and there is a net of elastic blood vessels at the base of the brain. Without these valves and elastic blood vessels, the blood pressure in the giraffe's head would be immense and cause brain damage when it bends over. As usual the creationist argue that such a complex series of changes would all have to occur simultaneously for the giraffe to "evolve' and this just fails to pass the test of "reasonableness." Darwinists have pointed out that all these changes occur slowly and incrementally, each change conferring a selective advantage to the pre-giraffe.

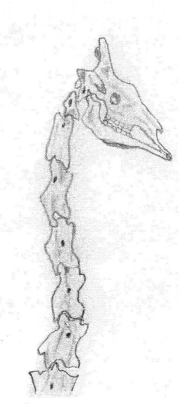

Giraffe neck

Most people assume that the advantage comes from gaining access to more browse at heights where other browsers cannot reach. This turns out to be unlikely because giraffes spend at least 50% of their time browsing on bushes below shoulder height. A more likely explanation is that the neck length confers sexual selection advantage. The male giraffes use their neck and head to battle for a female in estrous. The weight of the head produces great momentum when being swung at the chest, ribs, legs, and neck of their opponent. This act, called "necking", can cause great injury and even death. This argument is somewhat similar to one put forward by Richard Dawkins and others who have suggested that one of the reasons that the human brain developed such great intellectual power was, amongst other things, to help men win women. Giraffes cannot express their intellectual desires, if they have any, because they do not possess vocal chords. Women tend to be attracted to a variety of things that only a well-developed frontal cortex could conceive and acquire. This attraction is probably an evolutionary development that has been selected for because those individuals capable of charming, dancing, singing, whispering erotic verse and all the other manifestations of our large frontal cortex also succeeded in securing a mate and propagating those genes capable of conferring the brain with these skills. Fortunately this large frontal cortex is shared by women hence they can discern flash from substance. The ability to acquire sufficient money (the ultimate concrete surrogate of Darwinian fitness in *Homo sapiens* society) to buy a Ferrari does not always mean that particular male will hang around to provide best advantages to the kids.

I do not think giraffes pose much of a threat to humans, this is not so for the next wild animal we shall encounter on horseback. Of course, one should treat any wild animal riding a horse with great caution, as one should any writer who writes a sentence like that.

There have been countless admonitions to writers as to how they can improve their craft. Here is Fowler of *Modern English Usage* fame:

Any one who wishes to become a good writer should endeavor, before he allows himself to be tempted by the more showy qualities, to be direct, simple, brief, vigorous, and lucid.
Prefer the familiar word to the far-fetched.
Prefer the concrete word to the abstract.
Prefer the single word to the circumlocution.
Prefer the short word to the long.
Prefer the Saxon word to the Romance.

The two most common languages I experienced in Africa are Kiswahili and Afrikaans. The Dutch say that Afrikaans is like children speaking Dutch. You always have to be very careful when one language group casts aspersions on another, consider the French. Oh, all right, let's not. Consider the English and their supercilious disdain for non-English people who have the temerity to use "their" language and in so doing mispronounce and generally miss-use the beloved mother tongue. As many have said, the beauty of English is its promiscuity, it has in the past, and to this day, borrows and uses words from virtually every language, appropriating them and in so doing gaining a hybrid vigor and the wherewithal to express the most nuanced of meanings. The Dutch disdain for Afrikaans seems to stem in part from the observation that Afrikaans has a smaller vocabulary than Dutch, and instead uses a phrase to express the meaning found in a single Dutch word. For example, the best rendition of *gob smacked* in Afrikaans is *Slaat my dood met 'n pap snoek*. Which, literally translated, means, knock me dead with a soft snoek. The snoek is a long, slender, silvery-bodied fish with sharp, fang-like teeth. It can reach lengths of 4 ft, and swims in the seas around South Africa.

Betsie Rood, whom we will meet again later as the author of a cookbook laying out recipes for ietermahogs (pangolins, or scaly anteaters) and mopane worms, has also produced a nice recipe for snoek bread, the snoek being the fish with which you might surprise a South African by knocking him dead with a soft one. By the way, should you ever find yourself in a fish market in Haut Bay or some other South Africa coastal village and should you also be in the market for a nice snoek be advised that it is the ultimate insult for someone to try and sell you a soft snoek. Not only is it a case of trying to unload sub-optimal goods but it is also a clear demonstration that the fishmonger has written you off as an imbecile, or worse still, a tourist. Come to think of it, that is tautologous. Should you wish to create a little taste of South Africa, here is the recipe for snoek bread, and remember, when you are at your local fish shop be sure you aren't knocked with a soft one.

Snoek Bread with Vegetable Sauce

- *1kg fresh snoek*
- *5ml salt*
- *Pepper to taste*
- *50ml cornflour (Maizena)*
- *500ml skimmed milk*
- *125ml cream*
- *15ml Worcestershire sauce*
- *25ml onion juice*
- *Grated nutmeg*
- *25ml dry breadcrumbs*
- *Lemon wedges and parsley*

Mince the fish twice and on the second mince; mix in the salt, pepper, and corn flour. Then a third time, mince the mixture at the same time adding the milk. Place in a food processor. Slowly add the cream as you process. Quickly process in the Worcestershire sauce, nutmeg, and onion juice. The mixture should have the texture of thick cream. Grease a 22x12x7cm bread pan. Sprinkle a layer of fine breadcrumbs on the bottom. Spread the fish mixture on top. Cover with a piece of tightly fitting aluminum foil. Place in a pan of hot water. Bake for one and half hours in a preheated 190°C oven. Remove from oven and stand for 5 minutes before turning out. Keep warm and garnish with the lemon wedges and florettes of parsley. (Betsie Rood)

I am neither a Dutch nor an Afrikaans speaker but I can say that the earthy consonantal vigor of the Afrikaans is very appealing to my ear.

Some prefer to bang out their tunes in a colorful, vibrant, and simple language like Afrikaans. I think, in spite of his Boer war experiences, Winston Churchill would have approved, after all, he said, *"Short words are best and the old words when short are best of all."*

My riding pal Jürgen is a consummate Afrikaans speaker having grown up on a farm in the Great Karoo. To hear him speak the language is almost like being on one of those ox wagons creaking its way north away from the Bleddie rooineks towards freedom and the Transvaal. One of my favorite words is ietermagog, pronounced *yea-ter-ma-hoch*. It is a scaly anteater or pangolin, a solitary animal, seldom seen, and only active at night. It's the sort of word that once you say it you have to say it again. Sometimes when one picks up a phrase abroad it has applicability, one can use it on almost a daily basis and feel a small frisson of competence, urbanity, and demonstrable respect for the natives of the country. Such is not exactly the case with ietermagog. On second thoughts, I can imagine finding it in one of those apocryphal phrase books that are often the substrate for situational comedies. For example, there might be an occasion for a phrase such as, *"Excuse me but there is an ietermahog in my sleeping bag."* Sadly, there would be use for a phrase such as "Do you have any pangolin scales?" for they are much sought after amongst practitioners of Chinese herbal medicine for the treatment of liver and stomach ailments.

One evening Nancy and I, together with Jürgen and his wife, Friedrun, were in a private game park on the border of the Kruger. A fellow named Lood, (short for Lodewyk), ran the place, using the term very loosely. He is worthy of at least a separate monograph entirely to himself. He was rather short and rather round with a walrsusy white moustache and a passing, but only at a long distance, knowledge of African flora and fauna. He carried a .375 Magnum with him on all forays from the camp. Close inspection revealed that the gun was neither clean, nor had it been recently fired. This was just as well because it would have dislocated his shoulder if he had tried to save us from a charging Cape buffalo.

Let me give you a little flavor of his exploits. We arrived at his camp, Pungwe, after a long hard journey. We were keen to take a shower, only to hear that there was no hot water. Oh, well, no problemo let's have a beer instead. The next day there was still no hot water. We went for a game drive and came back to no water. Jürgen now assumed his imperious Afrikaans lawyer mode and tore Lood off a strip. We retired somewhat appeased by promises, which, in truth, none of us believed. The next day there was a great commotion caused by a fellow working on the well, which, by the way, had been knocked over by elephant. Lood looked pleased and said this chap was the best well fixer around. Our mild encouragement at this assertion caused us to enter into a conversation with Lood concerning the well. "Oh, is he really?" we asked. "Yes, definitely", replied Lood, "he used to be a mango salesman but found he could make more money fixing wells." That night we still had no hot water.

One hot water-less evening we were out on a game drive with Lood when we came across a lovely porcupine walking down the trail. We were admiring the animal when Lood said that on a night, similar to this, he was out driving when he saw a scaly anteater, an ietermagog. As soon as he had uttered the word, we all started saying it because it sounded so good. Before every subsequent game drive, we said we wanted to see an ietermagog. After a few outings, this became very boring, as I am sure you are strongly echoing. However, for me, ietermahog became an icon for the beauty of Afrikaans.

That night, after seeing the porcupine, we were sleeping soundly in our tent when all of a sudden water started pouring through the roof. In all the to-ing and fro-ing over the water, someone had buggered the float valve in the rudimentary water tank perched over our tent. I leapt out of bed bellowing for Lood. Lood, by his own recounting, bolted straight out of his bed and grabbed his rifle, convinced that a snake had bitten me. I can only thank the fact that I was born on the sunny side of the hedge that by the time he arrived one of the camp staff had a light on the situation or I am sure Lood would have blasted away at any snakes or Freudian look a likes.

A LITTLE BLOAT

We were approaching our final campsite at the end of this first Kenyan safari. It was in a bend in the Mara River, some 10 miles north of the Maasai Mara reserve. As we approached the Mara, we could see a deep pool in the river bend in which a large bloat of hippos were bobbing around. Collective nouns are wonderful and a sadly underutilized facet of the English language. Amongst my favorites are: A muse of capons; a wake of vultures; a flange of baboons; a troubling of goldfish; a bike of bees and a murder of crows. A bloat of hippos is not a happy occurrence when on horseback. In fact, I am thinking of pinching the goldfishes' moniker as the new collective noun for hippos when seen on horseback. The first reason to be unhappy when you see a "troubling" of hippos is that hippos kill more people in Africa than any other animal. Well, at least that is what people often sententiously drop into conversations whenever hippos come up, as if you were a local nincompoop who needed to get out more…"Oh yes, didn't you know that hippos kill more people than any other wild animal in Africa?" Upon careful research it turns out there are no data to support this claim, but it does make for a nice little anecdote.

The second reason that hippos are bad news is because they can run 18 m.p.h. whereas humans, even when the shit has been scared out of them, for example when being chased by a hippo, can usually only manage 12 m.p.h. Of course, you can go faster on a horse and hippos cannot jump. So should you be pursued by a hippo, keep calm and have the presence of mind to put a hole or a tree stump between you and the hippo. This advice is right up there with kicking black rhinos on their upper lip and poking crocodiles in the eye.

In spite of the hippo being able to run faster than us, there is something even more disconcerting about being in water with a hippo especially when you are on a horse since the latter, unlike hippos, don't spend a lot of time running in water. After all, the name hippopotamus derives from the Greek *hippo*-river and *potamus*-horse. It is not widely appreciated but hippos actually run on the bottom of rivers and pools; indeed, in droughts you can see their tracks on the bottom of the pools where they have been running around. So there we were on the banks of the Mara contemplating the forgoing facts and eyeing the distance we had to wade our horses and the steep incline of the opposite bank. Mark simply starts in and the hippos all turn to look at us. This was a relatively small bloat, containing perhaps ten, or so animals. To experience a better appreciation of the hippos' collective noun you should visit Katavi in Tanzania. Katavi is one of the most splendid parks in Africa. It is very isolated in Western Tanzania and is only accessible by a three-day drive from Arusha or a private plane. There is only one tented camp and the park of a million hectares only receives about a hundred visitors a year. The park boasts the largest herds of buffalo in Africa. Oddly Katavi is also home to millions of mice around the edge of the Chada flood plain. We were there, we saw two bloats, each of which contained more than three thousand hippos. They adopted a sardine like arrangement in viscous black cotton soil mud of Lakes Chada and Katavi. Every few seconds one would crowd another a little too much and set off a round of grunting and jawing in which they opened their cavernous mouths to display some fine teeth, which looked very much to me like those of *tyrannosaurus rex.*

As my riding compadres waded into the Mara I watched the hippos' little piggy ears twitching above the water and their huge noses bobbing at the surface. Occasionally one would give us a delightful grunt, the sound reverberating through its body and the water and seeming like a smug laugh, and then it would resume watching. Much like the explorer's party trekking through the jungle, being last in line is not a good place. So there I was, watching my comrades go in, wade across, nearly fall off trying to get up the bank and all the time I'm thinking any minute these hippos are going to have had enough of this and try a run at us. In I went keeping my eyes fixed on the opposite bank being very careful not to eyeball one of the hippos. Fortunately, the hippos kept on bobbing and I got across and even managed to get up the bank. It was only when we were safely at the top of the bank that Mark told us with his usual phlegmatism that on the previous safari one of the punters had got out too early on a soft part of the bank such that his horse did a back flip in the river and catapulted the rider in as well. Fortunately there were no hippos on that occasion which is just as well otherwise he may have become an example of the aforementioned and oft-cited anecdote about hippos chomping humans.

You may have wondered, as I often have, as to why hippos always look pink around the edges. I seem to remember hearing that they could get sun burned and I suppose sub-consciously I had assumed this pink tinge was the result of some foolish lolling around under the equatorial sun. Not so, hippos secrete a liquid onto their skin that protects against the sun. This substance comes from the hippos' sebaceous glands, starts out colorless, and turns red as it polymerizes. The structure of the compound has recently been determined and shown to possess antibacterial properties. There must be a great commercial opportunity here. Can't you see the advertisements "Try hippo block—tested by millions of hippos over tens of millions of years under the fierce equatorial sun of Africa—fixes your zits too!" I have just the logo for the company. I saw it on the side of a hotel in Windhoek called Hotel Christoph. We stayed there for one night on our first trip to Namibia. It was owned by a German couple recently emigrated from Nuremberg. For some reason they painted a hippo in a blue tutu on the outside wall of the hotel, I think this would look great on a tube of hippo block. This delightful tribute to taste continued inside. For example, in the dining room everything was squeaky clean amidst a fascinating mixture of Bavarian Kitsch that looked like a cross between my great Auntie Bertha's living room and a Third Reich beer hall. The black-backed jackal skin adorning the wall was balanced, perhaps even contrasted, with a budgie in a cage and German beer steins, the whole ensemble being topped off with a cuckoo clock. A sojourn in this place is a must should you venture to Windhoek. It is located on Robert Mugabe Strasse, how's that for another unfortunate fusion of German and African cultures?

We had another interesting encounter with a hippo in 2001, when we were in Kenya, again with Mark. We were riding by the side of the Mara River when this God-awful smell enveloped us. It was a dead hippo lodged in the middle of the river against a tree trunk and surrounded by crocodiles. Crocodiles cannot chew therefore they had to wait until the hippo rotted enough to split open and then they could tear off a piece and swallow it. Crocodiles also cannot move their tongue which is probably why they don't ask someone else to split open the odd hippo or two. As we stood there on the banks the already rotund hippo seemed to swell with the gasses of decomposition and we half expected it to explode in a mass of flying entrails and frantic crocs—alas, this spectacle must have happened later as we had to leave hippo and crocs as we found them—waiting. The smell of the hippo did not leave us entirely for Mark was wearing a bangle made from the hide of a dead hippo, which he had encountered some weeks before. In spite of the elapsed time, this charming little memento gave us a clear olfactory reminder of its putrefying cousin in the Mara.

Mark may not have been so enthusiastic about his new bangle had he been to the Museum of Modern Art in New York and seen Paul Thek's exhibit "Hippopotamus Poison" portraying a section of hippo skin in a vitrine, on which is written, "There is a conspiracy to poison the world with an extract of hippo skin."

4

Do You Have This Horse in Any Other Color?

Horse sense is the thing a horse has which keeps it from betting on people.

—W. C. Fields

So far, I have talked about the competence, or lack thereof of riders, well at least Gerry's and mine, as being a source of some danger. I have also spoken a bit about bad luck, as in Sabine's case and about the competence of the African animals in their ability to give you a run for your money. Now, much as in real estate location, I come to the three most important factors in African horse safaris—the horse, the horse, and the horse.

The very concept of me choosing a horse is a terrible conceit. Firstly, I am singularly ill equipped to do it since I lack both equine knowledge and experience; secondly the whole operation is carefully controlled by the guides who, in most cases, care about your health and well-being (note the insertion of the qualifying sub-clause) and thirdly, the horse invariably chooses you.

The method for selecting (a.k.a getting assigned) a horse is rather like finding a partner at a high school dance. The punters (boys) approach the horses (girls) with a lot of nervous chatter and bravado. Tales of former mounts and "bad draws" are bandied around. The horses for their part, having seen it all before, cast wary, experienced, and knowing looks at the punters. Onto this charged scene strides the safari leader (officiating parent). He or she is an expert in child and horse psychology. The substrate they have to work with is unusual. Before arrival, most horse safaris ask you to fill out a form outlining your previous experience. Punters invariably overstate their competence in the hope of getting a decent draw, namely a horse that will go but not kill them. The safari leader knows this and discounts the information. He casts a knowing eye over the punters, listens to their self-described skills and matches steed with punter.

A particularly poignant moment for me in the trauma of horse selection occurred not in Africa but in the foothills of the Andes in Ecuador. We had gone to ride on the volcanoes outside Quito. We arrived at the hacienda of the daughter of a former president of Ecuador. Her husband, Alphonse, was a romantic and had beautiful Andalusians. We were all assigned horses, one by one, and like the pimply, shy boy at the dance, I was the last to be matched up. I approached my horse and it promptly reared up like Silver on a Lone Ranger outtake. I backed off and tried once more with the same result. I then told Alphonse, no way José (as it were). I came to find out that he routinely injected all his horses with testosterone before arrival of guests "just to give them an edge"!

Back in Africa the aspiration of every punter is to get that mythical creature, rarer than a unicorn, namely a horse with nerves of steel, a kind, gentle demeanor, a lovely walk and trot and sure footedness above all else. It is difficult to discern these attributes by inspection from the ground. However, one can infer their absence by the presence of, amongst other things, lion claw marks on the horse's rump. This is usually a very good sign that the horse is going to be a bit edgy. This is not too surprising; you would probably be a bit edgy if you had been jumped on by a lion that then left his claw marks in your buttocks. Another good indication that you are in for some fun is the way the guides describe your horse. Here is a little phrasebook you may wish to copy and take with you on your next trip.

Guide speak	English
"He likes to be in front"	Uncontrollable
"Watch out for X"	X will kick the shit out of you
"Don't let him paw the ground"	He will roll over every chance he gets
"Keep your leg on"	He won't move unless chased by a lion
"He's a little shy"	Has been chased by a lion
"He's got a lovely walk"	He has a terrible jog-trot
"Be light on his back"	He will buck if a fly lands on him
"This is his first year carrying guests"	God help you

Once horse and punter are paired, there is the exploratory ride. The guide usually describes this as the time for you to get to know the animal (that will deliver you safely from the jaws of death) with the implied promise that if you don't like the horse you can switch it. We all quickly realize that some one else will then be stuck with it, you will become a pariah, and labeled incompetent by all your new-found riding pals.

Only once did we experience a pre-ride test of our skills, apart from Cindy and Tristan's gallops around Deloraine and this was in the Tuli Block in Botswana. The Tuli Block is generally referred to as hardveld because of the many sand-stone, granite, and dolerite outcrops and rocks of all shapes and sizes. The Block is 10 to 20km wide and 350 km long and was originally land ceded in 1895 by the Ngwato Chief Khama to Cecil Rhodes' British South Africa Company for the construction of a railway from the Cape Colony to Rhodesia (now Zimbabwe). It runs along the southern border of Botswana with South Africa. The railway plan was eventually abandoned, as it was decided that there were too many rivers to be spanned.

The Tuli strip is home to a lovely park called Mashatu linking into the huge, recently formed Peace Park, or The Great Limpopo Transfrontier Park—which straddles parks and sanctuaries across the borders between Mozambique, Zimbabwe and South Africa and includes the Kruger National Park—covering about 35,000km^2.

Mashatu is famous for its elephant herd, some 1,600 at last count, and it was amongst these animals that we came to ride.

We were assigned horses and my draw was Frankenstein. The guide was Steve Rufus, an experienced horseman from Zimbabwe who really knew his stuff. He had been driving by an abattoir in SA when he saw Frankenstein literally stand-ing in the killing line, he was fourth in line to be shot, and Steve bought him there and then for meat price. He is a 17h 1" paint with some shire in him. One eye was a soft brown, the other sky blue surrounded by a wide ring of white cor-nea. To my shame, I was not exactly enthusiastic about Frank when I first saw him. However, once I was in the saddle there was no better horse on earth as far as I was concerned. He was fast, safe, with a lovely trot (no jogging) and he was eminently sane. I fell in love with this horse.

Ian and Frankenstein

Once we had all mounted and ridden a couple of miles Steve took us into the dry riverbed of the Limpopo. Kipling's great, grey-green greasy river was now bone dry since it was winter and we ambled along its sandy bed.

The banks rose up on either side and we were soon some 25 feet below their tops. At this point Steve had us line up in the center of the river with our backs to the riverbank. He then called us by name and asked us to gallop up the bank. There was much dust and heart pounding and one or two ran some good distance before coming to a halt at the top but we all made it up in good order. The purpose of this test was to ensure that if we rode into a herd of elephant in the river we could all execute a sharpish escape. Once on the top of the bank, we regrouped and Steve selected a bush about 100 yards away. While the rest of us looked on, each person had to canter to the bush, ride around it, gallop back, and stop the horse in the middle of the on-looking posse. This was great fun and of all the punters, there was only one unfortunate who was a little iffy but he was good enough to continue with the safari. Unintentionally he made us all feel better, under the probably false assumption that if there was a problem he would fall off and whatever had caused the problem would eat him and not bother with the rest of us.

I respected Steve for this test and upon questioning; he told me that he had failed two people in the past. Both had overstated their qualifications and failed the test. He said with so many elephant around it was just too dangerous to risk someone falling off and getting themselves trampled.

I noted that throughout the trip Steve would invariably choose the steepest decline to get into the riverbed. He would rush down and then turn his horse around to watch each of us take the impromptu test; I always felt he was hoping for a dramatic dismount.

Down the banks of the Limpopo

I really appreciated Frank's qualities when we encountered our first elephant herd. We came upon them some 200 yards distant. There were about twenty elephants walking towards a water hole. Their walk is a gentle amble in which they articulate the ends of their legs as they pick them up and put them down in the soft sandy earth. They seemed to take no notice of us for a while and then, when we were about a 100 yards distant, they stopped, curled their trunks in the air, and turned to face us. The matriarch came forward, flapped her ears and trumpeted. Frank stood completely still with his ears pricked towards the matriarch. The magnificence and presence of this wonderful animal mesmerized us. After a few minutes, she decided that we were no threat and proceeded to amble back to the herd and on to the water hole. At this time we noticed another twenty of so elephant approaching from a different direction and soon they were all wallowing in the water, sucking up huge trunk-fulls and blowing it over their backs.

5

Loose Horses, Wild Animals, and Bad Holes

It takes a good deal of courage to ride a horse. This, however, I have. I get it at about forty cents a flask, and take it as required.

—Stephen Leacock, "Reflections of Riding", Literary Lapses

This is a tough section to write, not because horses are such noble and gentle creatures that are tolerant and easy to mind meld with but rather, as any owner will tell you, anything can spook a horse. Africa holds all kinds of possibilities to expand this "anything" category. The ones I have chosen to discuss are those that I have experienced personally and with some force. I should caution prospective riders in Africa that the list is not exhaustive. It is hard to know what will spook a horse. On your home turf, it can be a hand moved too quickly, a piece of cloth blowing through the stable or the clang of a water bucket. In Africa, there are more certain causes. They are, in order of spookiness to horse and, I suspect, rider: lions, site thereof, elephants, smell thereof, camels and finally anything that jumps out of the shoulder-high grass and runs making a noise like a hula dancer wearing a beaded skirt or, put another way—rustling grass.

When you touch a horse and run your hand over its skin you can feel the power, strength, and weight. Bring your hand to your nose and smell it. Smell that life, smell that pagan force. Take hold of a bridle after you have ridden your horse through the African bush and pull it through your fingers. Smear the paste of red dust and horse sweat on your skin and become a mundunugu, a witch doctor, a seer, and a sage. Lean forward in your saddle until your head lies on your horse's neck and feel the heat, taste the smell and smell the warm salt on your tongue.

LIONS

I know, I know, I can hear you saying "horses afraid of lions? No shit Sherlock." However, until you have ridden a bush pony with claw marks on his rump or seen the tawny eyes looking at your mount (or you and your mount) as supper it does not quite hit home. Lion stories are legion and all the best (or worst, depending on your point of view) tend to have happened on the previous ride. For example, the group before our first ride in the Loita Hills had been walking though grass in single file. A lion sprang upon the last horse in line and knocked off the rider. Mark was on the scene instantly cracking his bullwhip and driving the lion off. Then there was the time in Botswana when a group of punters was in a fly camp and a pride of lion surrounded the camp and roared all night long 5 feet from the perimeter. The noise was so loud that the tent wires vibrated: the horses were not happy. Fly camps by the way are not named for the insects that plague you but rather for their temporary nature. In bygone days people used to take the fly sheet from their main tent and use it to rig a temporary tent when going out on an overnight trip. I have already mentioned the story about lions attacking the horses at night as they stood tied to the long line and by the time the Maasai guards had driven them off a couple of horses were in bad shape. Fortunately, a vet was amongst the punters and he stitched them up. He did such a good job that my wife was able to ride one of them, Humpty, on her first safari. Sadly, Humpty succumbed some 10 years later to African Horse sickness.

Horses are not the only animals to be fearful of lions; humans tend to be a little nervous around them too. I experienced a dramatic example of this on my first trip to Kenya. We were riding by the Mara River. The early morning sun made the Mara valley glow with golden green light. We were riding down the side of the valley towards the river, which we crossed at a simple ford. We then ascended the Soit Oloolol escarpment on the west bank of the Mara. It is at the top of this escarpment that the scenes of Denys Finch-Hatton's funeral were shot in "Out of Africa." Finch Hatton was Karen Blixen's lover, Blixen being better known by her pseudonym Isak Dinesen, under which she wrote "*Out of Africa.*" She was introduced to Finch Hatton at the Muthaiga Club in April 1918. Finch Hatton was a handsome and gracious man. He shaved his head as a prank whilst at Oxford (where he had the distinction of earning a Fourth class degree) and his hair never grew back properly; he was completely bald at the age of forty. He farmed in Africa but spent most of his time hunting. He eventually sold his farm and lived in a small cottage on the grounds of the Muthaiga Club. He moved in with Dinesen in 1925 after her divorce from Blor Blixen. Hatton died in 1931 when his Gypsy Moth airplane crashed after take off in Tsavo. Dinesen buried him in the Ngong Hills and legend has it that lions sun themselves on his grave.

We followed a very narrow game trail up the steep incline strewn with boulders and thick with thorn bush and yellow fever trees. Suddenly a woman in our group fell off her horse as if she had been shot. She was shaking and convulsing on the ground and we thought she had damaged her head in the fall. Instead, she was an epileptic; even something as ordinary as this creates a real problem when you are many hours from a tented camp let alone medical help. Mark elected to ride back to our camp and bring a Land Rover as close as he could and asked that we stay where we were. By the time he said this we had been there about half an hour and, being such intrepid explorers, we all started walking off into the bush, having tied out horses to the nearest tree. Mark quickly appraised the situation and said in his famously understated manner that this was good lion country and we might get some clear sightings. I have never seen ten people move together so quickly. The magnetism of our fear sucked us into a single body with all of us facing outwards like Custer's Last Stand and nervously affecting indifference to Mark's comment. We remained quite close to one another until Mark returned a few hours later.

CAMELS

Camels are an unusual hazard since they do not occur in the wild in East or South Africa, indeed they were first introduced into Africa in the second century. However, they are very popular farm animals and as a result, we encountered them while riding through the farms of Laikipia surrounding Mount Kenya. It is hard to credit that horses do not like camels and I am sure there are people reading this who can look out through their kitchen window and see their horse and camel nuzzling each other. Nevertheless, let me offer a word of caution, that should you be riding in Kenya or Namibia and someone mentions that you may encounter a camel, beware. As we were riding one of my fellow punters, Caroline a doctor from Sussex, told me the story of a safari the previous year during which Tristan had warned the punters that they might encounter camel. Sure enough, as they came down an escarpment they ran into a herd of camel. Tristan ordered a dismount by which time the horses were jumping around and generally acting afraid, following which one woman lost control of her horse and he ran off. After much swearing and searching Tristan left the woman and rode off to camp with the safari, only coming back some five hours later to pick up the horse-less woman. That experience taught Caroline to hold onto her horse if camels were in the offing.

On the other hand, camels can be a delightful experience on safari. The next time we were back in Laikipia Nancy went on an early morning ride to a camel boma where they were milking the camels. The fresh camel milk was like a sweet latte, kind of an Africa Starbucks.

TALL GRASS THAT RUSTLES

On to the most often experienced "anything that jumps out of the shoulder-high grass and runs making a noise like a hula dancer wearing a beaded skirt." My own encounter with the latter happened when I was particularly enjoying the view from atop my horse as we walked through the tall grass of the Okavango Delta in Northern Botswana. The brain blasting beauty of the air, the dust, the smell of horse sweat, the creak of saddle and the flight of a trogon all mesmerized me. The grass was golden red and as we followed a game trail through it, a waterbuck decided that he was not going to wait this one out and decided to make a run for it. A waterbuck is about 600lb and when he makes a run for it, the grass tends to move. When this happed my horse rose straight up in the air about one foot and then, like the mouse in a Tom and Jerry cartoon, seemed to gain traction in mid air and lurched five feet to the side. It did not so much jump as teleport. For my part, I was sure this was it, and that I was about to be eaten and thrown or thrown and eaten. But no, it was just the ole grass rustle response to an ungulate. After which my horse simply took his place back on the game trail and resumed walking as if he had simply shooed away an annoying tsetse fly instead of leaving my heart on the trail a few yards back.

HOLES

Africa is shot through with holes. When I first went I thought about savannah, elephant, Maasai, and dust, but I didn't think about holes. Most people who go to Africa tend not to think about holes because they are riding around in Land Rovers and a Land Rover tends not to worry about holes unless they are bigger than its wheelbase. Not so horses. Horses do not like holes. A horse can put its leg in a hole, break it, pole vault you into Dante's inferno and if you aren't dead after the fall wait until you bounce in the back of a Land Rover for a day or two on your way to the local hospital where the MRI machine is not in crackerjack order. Hence, when you are on horseback and about to engage in a gait beyond walk you had better pay attention to holes. As Mark, our phlegmatic, and impervious safari guide would say before every canter, "Help your horses." Help your horses? Shit, who is helping me? I can barley stay on this SOB when it is barreling along some game trail. How the hell can I help him? If he doesn't see the hole then, to put it mildly and with the greatest restraint, we are totally fucked.

On my first safari, I was not a good rider and thus not a happy one. I clearly remember we were in the gorgeous rolling Loita Hills of Kenya and had just seen Colobus monkeys. Our guide was the taciturn Mark.

As I recounted earlier, my first canter with Mark resulted in me falling off as we came down from the canter to a trot. Later, on the same poignant trip we had had a wonderful afternoon ride during which we saw elephant, cheetah, and bowerbirds. As we were heading back towards camp the light was fading and we came onto a lovely open plain, sloping gently upwards, in other words a canterable piece of turf. Unfortunately, I had worn my prescription Ray Bans, just to look damn cool. The sun was going down and things began to take on a darkish tinge. Nevertheless off we went. It was the usual start, everyone spread out over the savannah and going like hell. Then I realized there were holes man, holes everywhere. My horse was doing well, dodging them like a bantamweight in an Olympic boxing match until we hit the mother of all holes. We both saw it coming. When I say hole I mean a warthog sized hole, big enough to swallow both a horse's leg and his rider's. Well I decided to go left, Top Brass decided to go right. I moved left he moved right. We then both simultaneously realized we were going in opposite directions, he moved left to try to save me, and I moved right. Somehow, we missed the hole but I shamefully brought all the other riders to a halt with my wailing. Nevertheless, amazingly I stayed on. I felt like those Indians in the Westerns, who hang on their horses' necks to avoid the gunfire. When I righted myself the adrenaline was coursing through my veins. We rode into camp and I dismounted, walked to the mess tent, and downed three gins. Margaret Thatcher's deceased husband Denis had a unique vocabulary for gins. It ranged from "An opener, a brightener, a lifter, a tincture, and a large gin and tonic, without the tonic, a snifter, a snort, a snorter. And a snorterino, which more or less empties the bottle in one go." Let us say I had three snorterinos. I think I was doing a good impersonation of David Niven in *Dawn Patrol*, who, having narrowly escaped being shot down, landed and went to the mess and had a gin or two to calm his nerves.

Ironically, the next time I fell off, I was a much more accomplished rider and was reveling in the chance to gallop over the wonderful plains of Laikipia. We were quite an expert group and the going was fast. The horses loved to take their head and move up from a collected hand gallop to a full bore charge. I was riding Mogwooni and we quickly clicked. My first injury on this ride came, as we were moving through some brush. I managed to get my cornea scratched by a wait-a-bit thorn. For those of you who have scratched your cornea you know this is not pleasant. The next morning I asked one of the syces to bandage my eye and off I rode with this patch looking for the entire world like a Napoleonic cavalry casualty. Forty-eight hours later, the scratch had healed and I could almost feel the final cells growing over the raw nerve endings and salving my pain. On the last day of the safari, we were all cantering along a wide track that comfortably accommodated two horses. I was behind Tristan and following him too closely. This is a cardinal error and you must not do it for the simple reason that with all the dust being thrown up you cannot see a damn thing. Sure enough Tristan jogged around a hole and my horse, Mogwooni, and I went into it full bore. Mogwooni did a forward somersault and I traveled some distance only to land on my shoulder. The impact completely winded me and as I came to, I tried to push myself up only to collapse back into the dust because I had no air in my lungs. This was distressing to those watching as they imagined I was a goner. Fortunately, I had broken neither limb nor spirit and managed to get back on but I felt like hell and had to ride the rest of the day like El Cid on Babieca, almost strapped to my horse.

The reason for recounting these minor tumbles is to assuage any fears you may have about riding in Africa being dangerous. Ha! Dangerous, its bloody suicidal but you do get to explore the edges of things, mostly your own soul as you keep saying to yourself why am I doing this. I remember reading Donald Morris' "*The Washing of the Spears*" on one safari and feeling tremendous empathy with the Brits who rode into Zululand and fell off their horse. There would be lines such as "Colonel Bugger-you-Smythe had to return to base camp having fallen off his horse"—ouch.

I have to throw in a quote attributed to William Faulkner, it is most apt for a book about horses; "I get drunk, I get mad, I get thrown from horses, I get all sorts of things. But I don't get edited. I'd rather see my wife get fucked by the stable boy." Not true in my case I hasten to add. As I write this, I would be happy to be edited.

Not all holes presage danger by virtue of their size. For example, there was the time when I was riding in Damaraland over one of the frequent plains, which afford superb gallops, and plenty of room to move out.

Galloping in Damarland

This was very advantageous because a group of us rode straight into a family of black mambas that were basking outside their holes enjoying the afternoon sun. We managed to split either side of the snakes but it was quite a thrill to see them loom up before us as we sped towards them. When you consider that black mambas happen to be the fastest-moving land snake in the world and carry the most lethal venom then you definitely need maneuvering room.

LOOSE HORSES

If you took all African horse safaris, distilled them down, extracted them with all the alcohol you consumed while riding them, distilled again, and then captured the very essence of what is left, do you know what you would have? Bloody loose horses. Loose horses. They run all over the place, cause falls, kick, bite, get lost, wont come when called (unless you can make a noise like a carrot) and won't clear off when sworn at. When a loose horse charged into us, my friend Jürgen would often yell his favorite phrase in Afrikaans *"Bleddie rooinecks en bleddie los perde"*—*"bloody red necks (a.k.a. Brits) and bloody loose horses."*

Of course, extra horses are essential, they are your spare tires, your alternative mount if you and your horse have a falling out, or off come to that. However, unlike spare tires you can't pack them in the Land Rover. They need to come with you in case you get the equine equivalent of a flat tire whilst on the trail. I well remember Lumpi taking a bent nail out of a horse's shoe during the ride across the Namib Desert. He used the indispensable and now ubiquitous Leatherman tool. For a more detailed discussion of the psychology behind the purchase and portage of this tool by latter day metrosexual frontiersmen see the section entitled *Haute Cuisine d'Afrique.*

Lumpi fixing a flat in the Namib Desert

At this point you may be asking yourself why the hell don't they simply lead the loose horses, I've seen Clint Eastwood do it a thousand times. Leading a horse at the walk is not difficult, however, when you move into a trot things get decidedly trickier, trust me, decidedly trickier. Unlike those Westerns where the high plains drifter seems to ride three thousand miles with a string of horses behind him, riding with a horse on a rope is not easy. So the solution is to let the bastards loose. This is when the fun begins. Horses have a pecking (or rather a biting and kicking) order and even when ridden, or especially when ridden, they prefer to maintain that hard earned order. Woe betide the neophyte rider who would rather huddle in the middle of the line if he happens to be riding Champion the Wonder Horse who would rather be number 1 or 2. Of course, the loose horses can go where they want and they do. They usually join the riding line at 30 m.p.h and an angle of 30°. This tends to unsettle the horses and their riders. The latter start yelling and screaming which the loose horses just love. These humans are such fun. So instead of staying inserted in the line they run off again, regroup and come in from the other side, maybe this time at 45° and 45 m.p.h. And so it goes, across the great African savannahs, or more especially the great African rocky game trails with little maneuvering room. I can honestly say, hand on heart, gin in hand that this is what African horse safaris are all about.

6

Oh How the God's Are Fallen

By this time, you may have the impression that safari guides are gods, sent down to spend a little time caring for lesser mortals before reclaiming their rightful position at the hooves of Pegasus. Much as Thetis forgot to dip Achilles twice in the Styx, all guides have their Achilles' heels, and over the years, I have seen a few.

The rider-less horse galloped past me, stirrups flying and with a determined set to its head that seemed to say, "At last, my chance to be in front." As I watched the horse, everything seemed to slow down as it does when you witness an accident. I have often thought about this phenomenon, and in my various riding safaris in Africa, I have had many chances to experience it. I think this perception occurs because your whole brain is focusing on what is happening. Perhaps this is an effect of adrenaline on the brain, selected for by evolution, which allows us to implement the best course of action when under threat. An old rowing friend of mine named Bob Zahringer told me that when he was a Navy pilot they were injected with adrenaline to see if their reaction times improved in simulated dog fights—they didn't, but it was an interesting idea.

Zen Buddhism urges its adherents to be present. This idea compels me; indeed all we have is this one moment, anything else, before or after, is a memory or a hope. As Jack Kornfield, our meditation teacher is fond of saying, "The past is just a memory, and the future is but a fantasy." He tells of a fellow teacher who has a sign on his office wall that he found in Las Vegas, it reads, "You have to be present to win." When you engage in exciting or dangerous pursuits you become present and experience all that life has to offer in that instant. As a result, time appears to slow down. It may be similar to the experience of young children for whom a summer's day is a lifetime. They are not freighted with decades of experiences that keep challenging and questioning everything they do. They do not create myths of anxiety about what they will do tomorrow or why what they did yesterday was not good. The ideal situation is to be able to keep doing this when you are neither a child nor in danger!

As I watched this particular rider-less horse go by me in the Kenyan bush, I started to think. The key word in the last sentence is <u>particular</u>. The rider of this horse was one of our safari guides. Safari guides are a breed apart, tough as a piece of biltong, encyclopedic in their knowledge of the bush and, well, thrill-seeking devil-may-care, live-for-today adventurers. But above all else, they are consummate riders. Africa is not a very forgiving place. It is tough on horse and rider and the terrain is riddled with potholes, snakes, and other hazardous material. The only thing that gives you any hope of making it from one end of a horseback safari to the other is that there are guides who do this all the time and are looking out for you.

Hence, my intense interest in this particular rider-less horse. The fact that it was one of our guides' horse, and the observation that it was now *sans* rider was indicative of a problem. I slowed my horse down and turned around. About 300 yards back, Beth lay on her back, motionless with the dust still settling around her. Slowly the rest of the safari reined in their horses and trotted back to her body. She still wasn't moving. Images of a broken back or worse filled our minds. The head guide, Mark, came up, and told us to leave her alone as he went to get her horse. Then, as if by force of will on our part she moved, she groaned, she propped herself on one elbow and groaned again. She was alive and intact—victim of a hole, winded, bruised in both body and ego, but ready to ride again.

We have already talked about the, to me, surprising fact that horses don't like camels. A camel keeps itself cool by continuously trickling urine down the inside of its back legs where the evaporation cools the blood near the surface of the membranous skin. I suspect horses know this and that is why they do not like camels. We were riding around the foothills of Mount Kenya, enjoying the unparalleled views with the mountain forming a constant backdrop. The huge ranches in the area create havens for all kinds of game and a few ranchers raise camels. As we rode through the small wait-a-bit thorn brush, we came upon a flock of camels. To our utter amazement, Mark's horse reared on its hind legs and promptly deposited him on the ground. My, the gods are mortal I thought, for Mark was indeed a god, if not the God. We have ridden with him four times in Kenya, and there he was in the dust, oh well *c'est la vie ou bien c'est la morte peut-etre?*

On this Laikipia ride, we had another guide fall. I say guide, when in reality she was one of the horse safari groupies. In this, as in nearly all cases, she was charming, kind, and not bad on a horse and generally good company. Most African safaris seem to attract these young women, ostensibly, it gives them a chance to experience excitement and learn something of Africa after school and before college. Arietta fell twice. The first time we were scrambling around in some god awful bush when her horse spooked and precipitated her on the ground not three inches to the side of a broken sapling. If she had fallen three inches the other way, she would have looked like one of Vlad the Impaler's victims, who, by the way is popularly thought to be origin of the Dracula myths.

The second time Arietta fell was due to the size of her breasts. She was well endowed in a delightfully natural way, I can clearly see her, and Nancy hamming it up with a pair of ostrich eggs, Nancy was the one holding the eggs. Tristan was quite taken with these (the breasts not the eggs). On returning from one ride a horse was lame but we were having a hard time determining which foot was affected. Tristan hit upon the idea (I am sure he had been planning this for days) of asking Arietta to trot the horse while we all looked (at the horse's feet of course). Arietta trotted the horse twice and we were no nearer making a diagnosis. On the third run, she put her foot in a hole and fell over. This of course gave Tristan license to examine her leg.

The guide's job involves trying to afford you some sense of adventure. The latter can become a little contrived, or at least it could in the days before everyone had a GPS, when it was not unusual for guides to declare themselves "lost." I could never determine whether this was true. It seems possible given that we often covered 20—30 miles in a day through bush and other terrain that did not afford many singular landmarks, but I suspected that they knew where they were most of the time. Moreover, who needed the adventure of being lost when we could break our back at any moment falling from the horse?

7

"Would you like the ostrich or the goat?"

The safaris we have taken have run the gamut from extreme luxury through notable privation. We have been alternatively parched, drunk, frozen, sweltering, hungry, unable to move and denied alcohol from periods of anything from about five minutes to a day. The Kenya safaris remain the best in terms of creating a sense of well-being while at the same time one of edgy adventure. Here are a few of the components that the safari outfits use to make you feel at home, or far from it.

TENTS

Home is almost invariably a tent. Tents, I have decided, are the best place to appreciate the third law of thermodynamics, namely that entropy is increasing. Any organized system that finds its way into a tent immediately becomes disorganized; this includes human thought as well as material objects. I think I have mentioned before the experience of arriving at the tent on the first night of a safari. I had carefully packed my baggage. Socks are resting in Velcro-sealed bags and carefully labeled "socks", ready to jump out at the drop of a hat. Upon opening my bag, I at first think there has been a switch at the airport. Nothing looks remotely familiar. I then begrudgingly accept that, yes, this is my stuff but that some over zealous custom's official or bomb inspector has rifled the contents into a Jackson Pollock look alike. Of course, none of this is true; it's just the weird air inside a tent, which renders me completely incapable of finding anything. Nancy would immediately enter the conversation now to say that the absence of a uterus underpins men's inability to find anything. This is a particularly painful assessment, in part because it is so overtly sexist but mostly because it is so true.

Another aspect of tents is that they keep you close to nature. The sounds of a shrieking tree hyrax or a roaring lion are definitely better experienced inside a tent than in a second floor condominium. On the other hand, this proximity does have its drawbacks. One night Nancy had to visit the long drop. This delightfully simple contrivance consists of a tripod placed over a deep hole on which is set a lavatory seat. As in all of life, balance is everything especially so when visiting the long drop at night. A torch is useful but it tends to tie up a hand and two hands are better than one on visiting the long drop. Perhaps it was due to Nancy not having three hands that she did not inspect the underside of the lavatory seat for blister beetles, and sure enough, she was zapped. There are over 2000 kinds of blister beetle and they contain a substance called cantharidin more commonly known as the infamous Spanish Fly. The Marquis de Sade was brought to trial for poisoning an entire orgy with Spanish fly in 1772. Because the biochemistry of this nasty blistering beetle is rarely understood, they are still used and misused by people today as a type of insect Viagra. Suffice it to say after crushing one of these beetles with her nether parts, Nancy was far from interested in the aphrodisiac aspects of blister beetles.

On another occasion, back in Kenya, Nancy had the misfortune to be bitten by a scorpion as we sat in the mess tent. We were well into our cups when all of a sudden Nancy cried out and started to rub her leg. Fortunately, we found the scorpion. Everyone was laughing and predicting dire consequences, about which I was not too happy. Eventually I managed to find out that it was harmless but very painful and Nancy spent a couple of days with one of the main nerves in her legs feeling as if it were filled with Tabasco sauce. She took a number of painkillers, however these only served to null the muscular aches and pains in her body allowing her brain to fix full force on the effects of the scorpion's neurotoxin, which was completely immune to the standard analgesics.

COME INTO MY MANYATTA

The West holds the Maasai in awe. They are physically beautiful with their high cheek boned Niolitic features and Giacommetti-like physique. Indeed studies have shown that most Maasai are as fit as Olympic athletes.

One day in the Loita Hills we arrived in camp at midday and Mark suggested we could visit a Maasai *manyatta*, the purview of one Lamaria. The manyatta was really an *enkang*. A round hedge of sharp thorn bushes form a stockade and its main purpose is to shelter cattle in an inner pen, also surrounded by fierce thorn bushes. The *enkang* may contain 10-20 small squat huts made from branches pasted with fresh cow-dung, which bakes hard under the hot sun.

Maasai huts are very small, with perhaps two "rooms" and not enough height for these tall people to stand upright or lie fully stretched. They are also very dark with a small doorway and tiny hole in the roof. The hole in the roof serves two purposes; it lets a little light into the hut but just as importantly it lets some smoke escape from the smoldering cow-dung fire which is kept alight for warmth and cooking—and perhaps to smoke out unwanted insects. Warmth may not be the first thing you would think of needing at the equator but most Maasai live at around 6,000 feet and in the absence of any humidity it can get quite cool at night. If you ever find yourself in an *enkang,* you will also find a million or two flies. The cattle and the dung attract them. The Maasai hardly appear to notice the flies as they crawl around their eyes and mouth. Indeed tradition has it that the flies represent the souls of their ancestors and it is very bad form to brush them away. I have however purchased a wildebeest tail fly switch and proceeded to swat at several thousand ancestral Maasai. It only occurred to me later to wonder why the Maasai made fly switches if the intended targets were indeed their ancestors' spirits.

Enkangs are sometimes called *manyattas,* both being collections of huts, however a true *manyatta* is really a camp used by an age-related group of unmarried warriors and may contain many more huts (built by the women-folk and set a short distance away from the *enkang*).

Cattle are the only things that matter to a Maasai. Recent genetic studies indicate that the Maasai migrated south into East Africa from Egypt, and that they probably brought the cattle with them. The purpose of every Maasai man is to amass as many head of cattle as he can. It reflects his worth and nothing gives him more pleasure than to watch these animals, know them individually, and enjoy the flesh and blood incarnation of his wealth. There is something to be said for this. We spend most of our time amassing electrons on a screen reflecting shares of this and that which we never touch or see and occasionally turn into geld for the acquisition of stuff we seldom really need. The appealing thing about cattle, as opposed to stocks and bonds, is that you can bleed them and milk them. Blood and milk, when combined in a smoke-disinfected calabash is the essence of life. You really know you are alive when you drink that stuff. It is complete, everything you need is there, and you still have your cows at the end of the day. Maasai believe that all cattle in the world belong to them, even though some may have temporarily found themselves in the possession of others. Thus, the Maasai have no compunction in raiding their non-Maasai neighbors in order to "return" the cattle to the rightful owners. Legend has it that Engai (God) had three children. To one he gave a spear so that he could hunt, to another he gave a hoe so that he could farm, but to the third, the father of the Maasai, he gave a stick so that he could herd cattle.

We arrived at Lamaria's *enkang* and he invited us inside his hut. It had two rooms, one for people, and one for goats. The presence of the goats lent a memorable smell to the hut. It fused with the sweat and smoke of the *enkang*. The walls were made of sticks, sealed with mud and cow dung. We filed in to the main room and because the fire was smoldering there was no light. The weight of the darkness was shocking after the brilliant equatorial sun outside. Mark interpreted our questions, effortlessly translating them into Maa and Lamaria's answers back into English.

I asked if I might take a picture. Lamaria uttered the Maa equivalent of "No problemo" and pow I pressed the shutter release. At atom bomb exploded in the tiny hut and Lamaria's wife's eyes were suspended in the blackness like chalcedony globes, fixed on me with a look of complete Zen presence, seemingly without emotion and yet intensely aware. I remember seeing a bronze bust of Apollo excavated from Pompeii, that had a black patina and white glass eyes. These were the eyes of Lamaria's wife.

We left the hut and were back in the dry mud of the *enkang*. Whilst we were in the hut, the women had quickly set up a display offering warthog tusks stained dark brown with tea, o-rinkas or throwing sticks notched and rubbed smooth with use and bead jewelry. I bought a snuffbox made from black buffalo horn with a perfectly formed leather top. When I open it, as I still do from time to time, I unleash the genie of Africa. The smoke, the dust, and faint smell of *naisugi* (snuff) roll through my brain. One of my other mementos of Kenya is a Maasai *nkarau* (calabash). The outside is the color of polished amber and has a patina of cow fat. Inside there are the remains of countless mixtures of blood and milk periodically sterilized by holding over a wood fire to smoke it or washed out with cow's urine. When I take the leather cap off, I can taste Africa.

What am I to make of buying these artifacts? For the Maasai they get money, something until recently they had no use for. Mark insists we bargain hard, which makes me feel churlish, especially when you are arguing the toss over one dollar out of two or at most three. The other thing is that you are carting off their heritage or heirlooms. I remember Berthuis, our pilot in Namibia, saying to me when I asked about buying what was obviously a very old necklace made from leather and bolts probably salvaged from a wreck on the Skeleton Coast, that if they wanted to sell it who were we to deny them that freedom. Of course, if we had not come, there would be no one to whom they could sell. The necklace would be handed down from mother to daughter. More importantly, they would have had no need for the money we exchanged. A few creased notes or small discs of copper are not terribly useful in eeking out a life on the Skeleton Coast. But then, we were there, as others had been before us. The genie was out of the bottle. I had my collecting/souvenir fetish to satisfy, they had acquired a taste for things only money could buy.

I have this terrible need to acquire physical mementos from my travels. I would like to tell myself that I am slowly outgrowing this need, however, it is a glacial process. I have often wondered what drives collectors. Fortunately, many, more capable than I, have been down this road and I am pleased to be able to reflect upon some of their insights.

Collectors, or at least collections, fall into two broad categories. One is those who seek to assemble a finite group, for example, all of Captain Sir Richard Francis Burton's books in first edition, and those who attempt to assemble some subset of an essentially infinite group such as china frogs. Some have argued that the drive to collect is just another form of materialism. I prefer the idea of control. Putting some semblance of order around a collection of things is demonstrable control. And yet, I think Philipp Blom has it best when he talks about the drive to collect as a way to try and stave off death. Blom goes onto point out that of course, in the end, death will prevail, and all the attributes that we sought in our collections will turn to dust along with us. Here is a closing paragraph from his book on collecting, "*To Have and to Hold*", in which he uses the maiden figure in the famous painting of Death and the Maiden by Hans Baldung Grien in 1510 as a compelling metaphor of the collector: "*The vanitas tableaux of Death and the Maiden have a durable erotic charge. They still seem to embody much about the nature of collecting in the face of the inevitable. The promise of love, which the Maiden represents, holds in it all the ambitions and hopes that seem to reverberate through collections over the centuries. Death hovering in the background…is the absolute denial and antithesis of all these qualities. The conquest is all his.*"

Werner Muensterberger draws a slightly different inference in his studies on the psychological underpinnings of collecting. He believes that most collectors need to re-stabilize their ego because of some early experience that left them feeling unsafe and not protected. This forced the child into avenues of self-rescue that manifested itself and lasted into adulthood in the form of the support of objects. Thus, the collector creates the illusion of a private and re-assuring world. Muensterberger goes on to say that objects in a collection substitute for close touch with a real person who was not available when needed as a baby. Indeed this further manifests itself in the display of collections that is really a simplistic way for the collector to gain vicarious love and approval through the admiration of the collection. Here are the final few sentences of Muensterberger's book (*Collecting: An Unruly Passion*) which capture his ideas succinctly... *"The Objects [the collectors] cherish are inanimate substitutes for reassurance and care. Perhaps even more telling, the objects prove, both to the collector and the world, that he or she is special and worthy of them."* This is fine and well for my collection of Captain Sir Richard Burton's first editions, but I am not sure what it says about your auntie's ceramic frog collection, or mine come to that.

I take solace in the ultimate dispersion of my collection and its re-incarnation in the collections of others. In this way, the books in it assume a Zen-like flow, moving in and out of collections like atoms moving in and out of life forms.

Our first visit to Namibia was in the form of a flying safari with the Schoeman family. Our guides were Bertus Schoeman and his wife, Helga. These were a delightful newly wed couple. Bertus is the son of the famous flying Schoemans who first started flying small planes into the Skeleton Coast as a way of accessing this remote environment. Bertus and Helga each piloted a Cessna 210, and before take off, they would lean out of their respective cockpits, and blow kisses to each other. I often wonder if they still do that today, I hope so. We flew from Windhoek's Eros airport to Sossuvlei where we walked on the 300' high sand dunes and then flew on to the Skeleton Coast. On one beach we landed in a 40 m.p.h. cross wind and stepped out of the plane to be abraded by a mixture of sand and seal fat being blown hard by the wind off the ocean. Along the beach were piles of diamond mine tailings and in spite of ourselves, we immediately began scuffing through the tailings looking for the next Cullinan. (This was the largest diamond ever discovered and was found in the Transvaal in 1907. It weighed 3,106 carats {that's 1lb 5oz}. The most famous diamond to emerge from the cutting of Cullinan was the Great Star of Africa, a 530.2-carat pear-cut diamond set in the British royal scepter). Alas, we found no diamonds, not that we would have benefited from them as they would all be the property of the De Beers Company that has the rights.

We had more success with agates. The beach was covered with them, rolled, and polished by the waves coming in from the Benguela current. Namibia is a geologist's paradise. When I was on the Damaraland ride one of the guides, Hanneliese, kept telling me that one could find the most beautiful topaz crystals just lying on the gravely surface. One day I spent two hours slowly traversing the desert in 90^0 heat looking for them. Lo and behold, I found the most beautiful amber topaz in the form of a hexagonal cylinder partially embedded in the hard gravel of the Namibian Desert.

In the end, I always assuage my concerns over the acquisition of artifacts with the observation that a bargain is struck and both parties are happy. Commerce as a surrogate for the Darwinian struggle continued and who was I to challenge or change that basic force? After all Darwinism is the Universal Acid. This is a term coined by Daniel Dennett in his book *Darwin's Dangerous Idea* in which he writes that his Universal Acid is an imaginary "liquid that is so corrosive that it will eat through anything" writes Dennett. He then goes on to explain the purpose of his book, writing, *"Darwin's idea…eats through just about every traditional concept…and leaves in its wake a revolutionized world-view…."*

I keep being pulled back to that. Most lay people (if they are not creationists) tend to think of Darwinism as the survival of the fittest and apply it to an animal population. In truth Darwin did not say this nor are his ideas restricted to the living world. Any process, which in changing (as all things do), if subject to an environmental pressure, will experience some selection. This in turn, will favor one process, and the entity that uses it, over another. I am often impressed and very sympathetic to friends and others whose work I read when they start going on about creationists. I used to become positively apoplectic myself, especially when they were banning textbooks or insisting that schools teach their particular interpretation of the Judeo-Christian story. This is an interesting phenomenon in a country like the USA that so strongly espouses the separation of church and state. Nevertheless, I have moved on and now see creationists as just another example of Darwinism in the raw. Here we have a group of people that, for whatever reason, have decided that their literal interpretation of the Old Testament must prevail. In so doing, they are setting up barriers between themselves and the rest of the (evil) world. Ideally, these barriers would lead to speciation, by which I mean that there would be no carnal intercourse between this group and outsiders. This would eventually lead to some changes, which over several million years might render interbreeding with non-creationists unsuccessful, this being the current working definition of speciation. Of course, many fundamentalist Christians have been caught with their trousers down, as it were, which just goes to show that strong as the creationists' belief is it is not enough to put a brake on sexual desire. In the end, the creationist philosophy will fizzle out because it confers no selective advantage, unless of course you are thinking of running for the presidency of the USA.

HAUTE CUISINE D'AFRIQUE

Men may lack a uterus but their coronary well-being is secured through their stomach, and stomachs are well catered to on horse safaris, well at least most horse safaris. The exceptions are notable only in a relative sense, the standard being so high.

Almost without exception, the food we have eaten whist on horseback safaris in Africa has been excellent. There have been some notable anomalies, especially in the Namib, and I have referred to these earlier, but on reflection, I think the spare diet on the trans-Namib ride reminded us of the severity of our adventure and helped to recall the Shutztruppe who pioneered the trail some 90 years earlier. In all honestly I must recount a particular treat which Lumpi delivered on that trans-Namib Desert ride. It sticks in my mind as one of the high points of the food I have eaten in Africa. It was not African food but rather frozen South African rhubarb with Bird's Eye custard. As with real estate, one of the most important things about food is location. The location for this delight was the side of the Gamsberg Pass to Walvis Bay road. This dusty track, along which we had been walking on horseback in 94°F heat, afforded entrance into the Namib Desert. We were close to sunstroke when we came upon Lumpi's yellow truck parked by the side of the road with an awning staked out to one side. We slid in to the delicious shade and were handed this heavenly combination of rhubarb and custard just starting to thaw—unsurpassable. In addition to the frozen rhubarb, Lumpi deserves culinary immortality for his smoked oryx. On first tasting this dish I quite enjoyed it. However, after the fifth or sixth outing, oryx or "rider's stew" as one of my companions liked to call it, began to pale a bit.

The benevolent view of safari food has to be due in part to its consumption in the open air after riding a horse all day, both of which are highly conducive to snarfing down the odd warthog steak. Talking of which I am still not sure how I feel about eating game. At one time or another I have eaten warthog, zebra, giraffe, eland, Cape buffalo, crocodile, and an ostrich egg omelet, although most of the fare is more tame. A typical meal we enjoyed in Kenya consisted of cold asparagus followed by baked Nile perch, spinach and broccoli followed by tree-tomato crumble all washed down with copious amounts of Tusker beer, wine and gins and tonic.

Tusker has become something of an icon of East Africa. There is seldom a book, article or anecdote about East Africa that does not manage to make an understated reference to Tusker. Understatement is key; the author or filmmaker has to create the impression that the drinker could have stood at the bar of the Norfolk Hotel in Nairobi in the 1930's, dressed in a crumpled linen suit. He would be lean, with piercing blue eyes, old beyond his thirty years and with a past filled with passionate Russian countesses, unusual sex and understated courage. When I first went to Africa, Tusker used to come in bottles with this label, which lent itself to the Great White Hunter mystique.

Tusker beer label

The origin of the name, and thus the label, lies in the history of Kenya Breweries, which was formally registered on December 8, 1922, by George and Charles Hurst. Their unique Lager beer soon became an East Africa tradition, allegedly being Ernest Hemingway's favorite. In 1923, an elephant killed Charles Hurst, and his brother named the beer "Tusker" in his memory. The company, seeking to shrive the colonial overtones of the original label and the beer, redesigned the label to show a cartoon of an elephant's head against a plain black background. There is another small label on the neck of the bottle which reads, in Kiswahili, *Bia Yangu Nchi Yangu*, which translates as, *My Beer My Country*.

Whilst we are on the subject of eating animals, I refer you to the book *Smulvleis uit die veld*, by Betsie Rood (of snoek bread fame) in which you will find a recipe to cook almost anything, including ietermahogs. These are delightful little fellows, which we met, at least in name, under the gentle auspices of Lood. Fortunately, for any ietermahogs running around your garden now, the book is only available in Afrikaans.

I asked my friend Jürgen to translate the book's blurb for me: I think it is a bit over the top.

"Do you have a terrible meat tooth? Then just certainly try these adventurous meat recipes. There is a tried recipe for almost every game animal—from roasted leg of wild pig to mopane worms. Or what about termites fried in pork fat, cooked scaly anteater (ietermagog)—or rice larvae on Melba toast? Don't shudder—its food fit for a king!"

Jürgen felt compelled to add this footnote: "Please do not try to cook and eat an ietermagog—they are charming animals and highly endangered!

Whist we are on the subject of African foods, the mopane worms mentioned above are a very big deal in Africa as a food crop. The mopane worm is not a worm but a large edible caterpillar that is an important source of protein and income to many people and forms the basis of a multi-Million rand trade in the Limpopo Province of South Africa as well as in Botswana and Zimbabwe.

The caterpillar feeds on the mopane tree and metamorphoses into a large and attractive Emperor moth (Family *Saturnidae*). Here is a nicely succinct method for preparing them, taken from the Transvaal Museum.

Mopane caterpillars are prepared for eating by squeezing out the gut contents before they are fried in their own body fat or boiled in a little water. Most of the caterpillars are dried so that they can be stored for use throughout the year. Dried caterpillars may be eaten as a snack or rehydrated and cooked in a little water before they are fried in oil with onion and tomato. They may be served with pap (maize meal porridge), or onion and tomato gravy and atchar (chili sauce).

One night in the Okavango Delta we were sitting around the fire enjoying our sundowners when the chef, delightfully named "Person", and married to the equally delightful "Tiny", came out with a bowl containing a barbell fish. The Okavango is renown for its barbell fish, especially as they provide food for the Tiger fish. We peered into the bowl and sure enough, by the light of the flickering fire, we could see a long fish-like object in the pan. We started to congratulate Person on his fishing skill but he modestly said that some local fishermen had caught it and brought it to the camp. We sat back into our chairs and continued our inebriated conversations on life, the universe, and the beauty of the African night. We were called to dinner and filed into the mess tent expectantly. Our piscatorial anticipations were soon changed as we watched Person slice the barbell fish to reveal succulent pink slabs of Cape buffalo tenderloin.

I must say something of the camp kitchens. The kitchen tends to be next to the staff tents and becomes a focal point for the staff when they are not working in the camp or tending the horses. It's a great place to sit down and relax, and get a bit of a sense of the life of the average African. The talk is largely about families; wives and children at home in the village, and when they will see them again. It is good. The kitchen itself is a pile of wood coals on which sits a grate supporting a frying pan or metal box. From these humble sources, the bush chef produces freshly baked breads, pies, and all sorts of English public school-like meals. The quality of the food is excellent and is cooked well, two major distinguishing factors compared to English public school food.

We have sampled a little rougher cooking. When I was in Tanzania, I spent some time with the hunter-gather tribe, the Hazda. The women would go off into the bush and dig up fibrous roots, which they would eat raw as well as throw them onto a fire, occasionally turning them before pulling them out and eating them. I tried one, it was juicy and fibrous. The more I chewed it the bigger its mass became. Soon I had a mouthful of fibrous pulp that I could neither chew, swallow nor spit out. A Hadza mundunugu had to extract it with a forked stick.

After visiting the Hazda, we spent some time with a Maasai group at Endulen near the Ngorongoro crater. Endulen is a school set up by a catholic missionary named father Ned. His intent is to provide Maasai boys and girls the skills to be able to enter the equivalent of a high school. For this they need basic reading writing and math skills. This is something that they could not get in the rural Maasai community. Father Ned's logic is that as the population of Kenya continues to explode there will be more and more pressure on the land. Those tribes that have members who can become lawyers and politicians will be more successful in obtaining land than those tribes that cannot participate in the legal and political processes. This is a compelling argument even though it does of course start to fragment the Maasai life style that has evolved over millennia to fit the land.

Roasted Goat

When we arrived, the Maasai celebrated our arrival by sacrificing a goat. The sacrifice, carried out with much ritual, served to remind me how valuable meat was and how important it is to offer food to strangers as a sign of respect and peace. They suffocated the goat by holding its mouth shut and then placed it on a bed of leafy branches. Very careful cuts removed the skin, followed by the subcutaneous fascia and each organ. The process reminded me of a student anatomy lesson. When it was finished the only thing left was the stomach contents, everything else had its own a specific use. The delicacy was the liver, which we sampled later in the evening. Cooking consisted of skewering the meat and liver on sticks and placing them in the earth in a ring around the fire, sort of Maasai goat kebabs.

After dinner, about 100 Maasai gathered around the fire and treated us to a bilingual story telling. Two young women, bedecked in beautiful blue robes and white beaded collars, stood up and told the story of Engai, the Maasai god, and how he sent a dog down from heaven. As the story unfolded, the moral became clear, Engai had powers that he had not shown to man and which man could not even conceive of. One girl told a piece of the story in Maa and then the other girl translated it into English. We sat, listening to their voices, amongst all the spellbound Maasai.

The next day we took a tour of the school at Endulen. There are some half dozen buildings and a schoolroom. They are very primitive and yet the children adore the place and take their opportunity to learn so seriously that I felt ashamed for taking so much of my own education for granted. We entered the kitchen. This was a 15-foot square building with an earth floor and no windows. Light came in through gaps in the walls where mud had fallen off the vertical wooden slats. In the center of the floor was a wood fire and resting in its coals was a large iron pot looking like a prop for Macbeth's witches. Inside the pot were pieces of yesterday's uneaten goat bubbling around to provide the children with their lunch.

At this time I would like to make mention of a piece of equipment which, as you will see in this instance, has a decidedly epicurean twist to it. There is a well-recognized and oft scorned proclivity of the intrepid African traveler to equip typically himself, as opposed to herself, with some sort of hardware that is redolent of what he imagines Captain Sir Richard Burton took with him when searching for the source of the Nile. Of course, with today's intense market-savvy businesses Leatherman came up with the perfect surrogate. A chrome steel tool with razor sharp knives, pliers capable of extracting the molars from a bull elephant and all kinds of other tools, absolutely none of which are of the remotest use to you when on a horse in Africa. In spite of its superfluity, this tool was enormously successful and much copied. Realizing this, Leatherman sought to expand its market by diversifying into a variety of niches. Amongst other things, they decided to come up with a tool without which your average metrosexual would not be able to survive. They called it the "Flair" and its key redeeming features (apart form its gold color accents and engravings of grapes on the side), are corkscrew, pate knife and cocktail fork. I promptly realized the value of this tool and bought one. Jürgen, my biltong-chewing buddy in Cape Town, has long had a Leatherman fetish and was fond of whipping it out and displaying its various tools to any unfortunate person who happened to be around.

Here is how I broke the news of my purchase of a Leatherman "Flair" to Jürgen:

Letter to Jürgen:

> *I did it! I bought a Leatherman—but—wait—not just any Leatherman. I bought the YuppieMan. It has, wait for it, I can see you turning green with envy…it has, are you ready, you better sit down, it has…I can hardly bring myself to describe it is so amazingly beyond your wildest dreams…it has, are you SURE you are sitting down? Well it has…no I can't do this to you, really, you are my friend, but I can't keep it to myself. Well here goes. It has…a cocktail fork!!!! A corkscrew…and, and this is the ultimate…it has a pate knife!!!!!! Haaaa eat your heart out, ha! HA ha ha Oh, I forgot to mention…it has pair of scissors too……….:-)*

And his reply:

> *Ian!*
>
> *How crass! How absolutely grossly revolting, typically capitalist envy-driven consumption of irreplaceable resources—the next generation will*

see the production of that abhorrency as the irreversible turning point in the final despoliation of our planet, and the collapse of Western civilization as we knew it! A pâté knife indeed! When what you really need in a survival tool built for the genuinely tough is a Wet-Ones dispenser, for wiping your arse when far from the nearest toilet. Now I have gone the other way—I refuse to compete when I know I cannot win. I have discarded my Leatherman Supertool, and gone back to the original version, which has only a knife and useless things like that. I can't wait to see this monstrosity of yours. Fortunately, it will be in the States, as you would not dare bring it to Africa!

Your horrified ex-friend Jürgen

In spite of Jürgen's protestations, I took my "Flair" to Tanzania and used it with aplomb, but not, alas, with a pâté.

Omelet

When riding in Laikipia in 2002 I had the great good fortune to secure my breakfast whilst on horseback. We had been riding for a few hours when I came upon a singleton ostrich egg. An ostrich egg is equivalent to 24 hens' eggs, which bodes well for the title of this section. Ostriches have the habit of laying singleton eggs from time to time and not incubating them. These eggs act as a decoy from the real nest. These nests are communal and contain up to two dozen or more eggs.

Ostrich nest

I picked up the egg and put it in my saddlebag, hoping that it was still fresh, and took it back to camp. Once there we blew the egg and had it as an omelet for breakfast. It had a wild, delicious, rich taste that fit with the smell and feel of the bush. I should say in passing that blowing an ostrich egg (which was done purely because I wanted the shell as a souvenir) requires a good pair of lungs. Tristan volunteered to start the process, but as his face turned from puce to purple, I took over.

It is perhaps not surprising that ostrich shells have many uses in Africa given their singular beauty. The shells are relatively thick and have a creamy ceramic surface contrasting starkly with their dry dusty environments. Bushmen have used them to carry and store water for thousands of years and in Damarland the women make necklaces out of broken ostrich shells, drilling small holes into the center of the fragments and rubbing them on their thighs to smooth the edges.

An ostrich can live for twenty-four hours without its head, which may be because an ostrich's eye is bigger than its brain. Upon hearing this, Gerry said he thought that if you cut Astrid's head off she would keep talking for twenty-four hours. For unrelated reasons Astrid and Gerry are no longer married. When I told Gerry that I might include his comment in this book, he sent me a note saying, "The remark that Astrid would talk for another 24 hours after her head was severed cannot not have come from me. I might have said something like that in a moment of alcoholic excitement and with my arm lovingly draped around her slender shoulder." By the way should you find yourself in the unenviable position of being close to a headless ostrich you may want to have four of five friends with you to hold it down. Apparently, they can run around *sans* head for a good 45 minutes.

As with all homes, the hearth represents that focal gathering point and in Africa, the fire has surely been one of the prime drivers for our cultural evolution as we gathered around it for warmth, protection, and as we used it to cook food. It may have been an important catalyst in the development of language.

CAMP FIRES

The fires on safari are amongst the most poignant and memorable images that I carry with me through the New England winters. One evening as we were riding in the Namib Desert we came to a halt in a vast open plain. The only break was a large stone kopje about 500 yards from our campsite. We dismounted and fed the horses and tied them up to the long line, strung between the supply truck and an iron rod pounded into the desert floor. We changed from our riding gear and repaired to the fire as dusk began to fall. I was restless and decided to explore the kopje. After walking on narrow game trails and watching the night fill the vacuum created by the dying light, I turned my head back to our camp. All I could see was the fire and a small group huddled around it. The sparks streamed into the liquid black sky and the low laughter of the group reached my ears as if through cotton wool. That scene is the one I tried to capture in this poem, written in my sleeping bag that night with the southern constellations turning over my head.

A Campfire in the Namib

The Sun hovers, shimmers and melts slowly into the desert.
I stop on a narrow path packed hard by the feet of Bushmen and gemsbok.
A sudden intake of breath breaks the silence of the last pale ochre light.
Color draining from a dying grandmother's cheek.

Thick night sky seeps into the silence with its deafening beauty.
Drops of breast milk squirted on black velvet

The weight of the liquid blackness presses down on me.
Each drop of milk belying my vanity.
I am nothing, nothing.
The spirituality of the Bushmen means nothing to this milk in the sky.
Scorpio's eyes transfix me with a sense of evil,
No, not evil, liberation, a complete disregard.
I am nothing, I am utterly free.

The flames of the campfire swirl in the tarry blackness,
I think of Eliot's country folk, my ancestors, dancing around another fire a hemisphere
away.
For once, it does not draw me.
How could it compete with the freedom of nightfall behind me?

A thousand generations ago four yellow skinned Bushmen sat around a fire,
Their ostrich eggs filled with life.
The flames dancing, their eyes shining with the magic of stories.
The hunt for an eland,
The death of a grandmother

As I walk back to that fire
I find a broken ostrich shell,
How I wish I had looked down and seen my own skin, yellow.

It must be in the genes that urge, even need, to sit around a fire, to look into the flames, and see your life roiling in the burning gasses. Perhaps it is the association with food. Perhaps it is the life-giving warmth or perhaps the ability to keep wild animals at bay or maybe the means to bring people together around the hearth. I think it is all of these. Moreover, around those prototypical hearths Man learned to talk, to pass on experience, to cooperate and to create culture. What other thing outside ourselves could confer all these advantages to our ancestors?

Domestic fire has held Man in thrall for hundreds of thousands of years. In more recent times, the ancient Greeks developed mystical and religious ceremonies to do with fires. As an indication of the importance they placed on the spiritual aspects of fire they recognized several aspects of a fire-based prophecy such as *pyromancy*—looking into fire; *capnomancy*—studying the passage of smoke and *spodomancy*—the examination of ashes.

Personally, I like the idea of haruscipation, that is the study of entrails, usually bird's, as a means to discern the future. Recently a group of scientists has sequenced the DNA of the chicken genome. This has to be the ultimate in haruspication, something that the ancient gazers into crow's entrails must have fantasized about because we can now compare our genome with that of a bird, the closest living relative of the dinosaurs. Surely, our genetic similarities must foretell some things of great moment.

A great campfire has to have the right setting. I have enjoyed fires in the Namib Desert, the Loita Hills of Kenya, in Laikipia with Mount Kenya on the horizon, and the Ugab River bed in Northern Namibia. The calls of hyena and the distant roar of lion echoing in the blackness of the night enhance the mystery and magic of the fire. The night's soft, rich, fragrant, tactile blackness suck up the sparks and smoke of the fire and the Milky Way appears almost three-dimensional, like drops of milk on velvet.

Enough of this pseudo-psychoanalytical claptrap. The essence of a good campfire in Africa is alcohol. A short stagger to the mess tent where there is a fully equipped bar, ice cubes and more gin than you can shake a stick at. The mixture of ethanol, flame, night, and the bush brings out the utmost bullshit from one's fellow punters.

Perhaps the flames act like a drug, one that alcohol makes even more powerful. Michael Pollan argues in *Botany of Desire* that psychoactive drugs such as cannabis are pleasurable because they confine you to the present by dissolving short-term memory. Could the flickering flames stimulating the visual cortex produce a similar effect? I tend not to reflect on my life or my future when looking into the flames. I find myself becoming present, perhaps the flames are able to simulate the effects of meditation in removing thoughts of past and future and centering our conscience in that moment allowing you to achieve some measure of the Zen grail of being fully present. I have said it before and I will say it again, the key to life, happiness, fulfillment, and meaning is being present, here, now, at this still point of the turning world. All you have is this one moment. The past is history and the future is just a fantasy. You have to be present to win. When you look into the flames burning in the African night you are surely present.

Hyena Fire

I remember a campfire in Botswana. We were in the Tuli Strip and had been riding amongst elephants for several days. We had pitched camp on the bank of the Limpopo and were sitting around the fire, reflecting on the day. We sensed a presence and there, not ten yards away, was a beautiful spotted hyena. Its head slung low beneath its shoulders with massive jaws and round ears. It just looked at us, as if contemplating whether to come in and take off one of our legs for its supper. It seemed the very incarnation of Dracula.

The perception of hyenas has changed enormously in the last twenty years or so. When I was a boy in England and watching wildlife documentaries hyenas were always portrayed as scavengers, stealers of food and generally to be despised. Even now, after many trips to Africa, the first metaphor I reach for is Dracula. Today, the hyenas PR is much better and most people think of them as fascinating hunters and powerful predators on par with lions. This change was started by Kruuk, a German scientist working in Ngorongoro crater, when he found that 60% of a lion's diet was taken from hyena kills. This study started to put the hyena on par with lions as *bona fide* hunters and not skulking scavengers. Nevertheless, maybe there is something else to this association with evil. Certainly, in African folklore, the hyena is associated with evil, typically as a witch's familiar. This is compounded by early beliefs that the male hyena mated with other males, probably the result of confusion in assigning sexes to hyena because the females possess an especially large clitoris such that the external genitalia are very similar. Perhaps the aura of evil comes from their galloping lope with their heads bobbing high over their shoulders. Perhaps it is the round ears, which usually portend cuddly toys and not the most fearsome jaws on the planet. There is an Ndau proverb: *Nothing that enters the mouth of a hyena comes out again.*

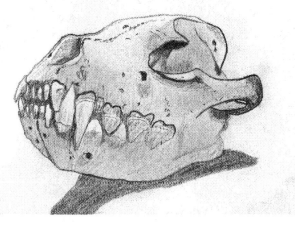

Hyena skull

For me the most compelling characteristic of the hyena is its cry. *The Good, The Bad and the Ugly* is the most famous of all of Sergio Leone's films, largely because of the Ennio Morricone score featuring its instantly recognizable other worldly howling. Morricone's theme was the attempt to recreate a hyena's cry. While most people probably don't recognize it as a hyena, its visceral power creates the perfect atmosphere as it recurs throughout the film. It is one thing to sit in a movie theater enjoying Clint, quite another to be in the African bush listening to *Crocuta crocuta* cry and feel the hairs on your neck rise. I digress, but I just love hyenas I think my affection is based on their round ears, the loping run, their toughness and that they are underdogs if you will pardon the metaphor.

I have seen hyenas from horseback but never been attacked by one. If I were, I would probably want to have William Cotton Oswell, along with me. He and Livingstone "discovered" Lake Ngami in 1849, and apparently, he could fell a hyena by undoing his stirrup leather at the gallop and knocking it on the head with the iron. I wish I had known this when I met Helen on a safari in Botswana. Helen fell off more times than any other punter I encountered on a ride. Fortunately the sandy soil of the Okavango Delta meant that she didn't hurt herself too badly, however as the days progressed she developed a certain stiffness and a noticeable limp. Her claim to a secure place in the African Horse Safari Rider's Hall of Fame was the most remarkable feat in which she galloped through knee-deep water and on coming to a halt with the rest of us promptly fell off. It was then that she realized she had lost both of her stirrup leathers. Stirrup leathers hook onto the saddle beneath a flap and are impossible to detach unless yanked backwards with considerable force and dexterity. Just how she managed to do this remains a mystery but I suspect it is due to a distant relationship with Mr. Oswell of hyena bonking fame.

Richard Leider in his book *Claiming your Place at the Fire* has captured the role of the fire in human social evolution. He believes it represents that place where elders are able to nurture the tribe, share learning, and act as counselors. I think we all recognize this experience. Whether it is from camp fires of our youth, or those fortunate occasions when one can sit in a house gazing into a natural fireplace with friends or the camp fires in Africa I have tried to describe above. Do flames open our minds in the same way as Huxley thought mescaline opened a valve in his mind to let the whole world of sensation flood in *Doors of Perception?* Does this mood allow the wisdom of the elders to exert its effect? If so what could be the modern equivalent of that fire? Alas, I think there is none, unless it is Starbucks.

8

West into the Night with Rank

Flight is but a momentary escape from the eternal custody of the earth...
I feel the wind rising and the rain falls hard. The smell of petrol in the cabin
is so strong and the roar of the plane so loud that my senses are almost dead-
ened. Gradually it becomes unthinkable that existence was ever otherwise.

—Beryl Markham "West with the Night."
On her solo flight across the Atlantic in 1936.

If you ride in Africa, the chances are very good that you will end up flying in Africa. Along with hippos killing more people than any other animal it is also popularly held that flying in small planes in Africa kills more tourists than hippos. Of course, if you find yourself assigned a seat next to a hippo you may want to ask for a different draw. I must say right up front that I have taken well in excess of 50 small plane flights in Africa and never had a single bad experience, except for the time I flew with Rank.

There is no sound so sweet as that of a prop plane heading your way as you stand on a dirt landing strip in the middle of the African bush. It is sweet because the planes are nearly always late and if they don't show up you are rather out of options. We were in Chelinda on the Nyika Plateau of Malawi waiting for a plane to take us to Windhoek in Namibia—a distance of 1355 miles. We had almost given up on this particular plane. The plane was delayed 2hrs by the weather and didn't arrive in Chelinda until 10 am. At last, we heard the thrum of the twin-engined Beechcraft and watched it land amidst a cloud of red dust. As the dust settled, Rank appeared from the cockpit. Rank was an ex-Air Zambian pilot before it went bust. He was a delightful chap full of laughter but with a rather catch as catch can attitude to life in general and flying in particular. A twin engined Beechcraft is a small plane for four people plus pilot, especially when two of the people are Gerry and me, each 190lb. Nevertheless we shoe-horned ourselves into the cabin after packing Gerry's diminutive wife Astrid into the taper-ing rear of the cabin on top of our copious luggage. Eventually we took off for Lilongwe where we went through a tortuous process to get our Malawi exit visas. We then flew to Mfuwe in Zambia to refuel. We had an impromptu lunch at the aptly named Mad Dog Café. I recommend this place unreservedly as THE place to eat in Mfuwe airport. No matter that it is the only place to eat in Mfuwe air-port. Three hours later, we flew over Victoria Falls and landed in Livingstone, named of course for the great explorer and missionary. He was the first non-Afri-can to see the falls in 1855 and there is a classic colonial statue of him looking out forever over *Mosi-oa-tunya*, the indigenous Kalolo-Lozi name which means "The Smoke that Thunders."

Rank had to go and wade through the inevitable paperwork and try to save us from having to pay some sort of extortionate landing tax. As he walked away from the aircraft, he asked Gerry and me to fill up the wing tanks, and to be sure that they were full because we would need the fuel. It may surprise you but this was our first experience of refueling a plane. After we saw the fuel bubble up in the wings, we rocked the plane gently to ensure there were no air pockets and that we had as much gas as possible. Having performed this feat totally unsupervised, we hit the airport bar where we had our picture taken by a local drunk. Sadly, Nancy and Astrid could not join in for reasons that will soon become clear.

Rank reappeared with papers and a halfhearted suggestion that we go. We repacked ourselves into the plane. At first, the engine wouldn't start, then only one landing light worked and then Rank didn't want to take us because we would arrive after dark. His exact phrase was "I am not sure we will make it." This is an example of his exasperating laissez-faire attitude. How could he only now come to the realization that we wouldn't reach Windhoek until after dark? It was on the other side of Africa for Christ's sake! Since we had reservations on a couple of Piper Cubs to fly us up the Skeleton Coast the next day we were in no mood for waiting so we told him we had to go and he had better get this thing off the ground!

As we flew Rank refused to turn on the heater in order to preserve fuel (which did nothing to increase our confidence about the flight!) so we were huddled in this freezing little plane as it flew into the western darkness. I should also add, some-what superfluously, that there was no lavatory on the plane so Astrid and Nancy were not happy, their situation not being improved by the cold. Cold weather makes you want to pee more because the cold increases your blood pressure. This stops the secretion of a hormone called vasopressin, whose job it is to inhibit urine production (diuresis), the end result is you end up making more urine and being very uncomfortable in a lavatory-less flight from Livingstone to Windhoek. Those of you not familiar with cold-induced diuresis will probably be only too familiar with alcohol-induced diuresis. The mechanism is similar in that alcohol inhibits vasopressin secretion. As a result, you end up getting up several times in the night after having been out on a bender. Furthermore, you are likely to wake up with your brain feeling like a shriveled walnut because of the dehydration. This loss of water is really the root cause of all hangovers. The sure fired way to prevent this is to drink a pint of water before you retire. Even though you will still have to get up in the night you will feel much better in the morning—trust me, from someone who might have had occasion to try this remedy.

During this freezing trip, Rank told me about his brother in Zambia who did a nice line in emeralds. I send him some money he sends me emeralds by Fed Ex; sounded good to me but Nance gave me the evil eye so I passed on this opportunity of a lifetime. I kept looking at the GPS, there were NO lights beneath us, and eventually we were some 20 miles from Windhoek and still NO lights. I felt sure we were going to crash land in the Namib Desert. Then Rank said he had to signal to get the lights on. All of a sudden, Windhoek airport lit up beneath us! Two teenage boys stamped our passports and then we cajoled a taxi to take us the 30km into Windhoek and the famous Hotel Christoph, which I have already described in the chapter about hippos. When we arrived at the hotel, they had shut up for the night. Shutting up in Windhoek is a serious matter and involves closing and locking metal gates topped with razor wire and letting loose the dogs. After much banging, a very suspicious night watchman came out and eventually let us in. Rank, true to form, had made no plans and was given a broom closet in which to sleep. By this time, we were all starving having shivered our way across Africa and we had that giddy bonhomie that comes from having survived a dangerous ordeal. We wanted to eat and were told that there was a German restaurant nearby that was still open. Therefore, the four of us plus Rank found another taxi and zoomed off into the night in search of, what we believed at the time, the improbable prospect of finding a German restaurant. Sure enough, we found it complete with eisbein, beer steins, and blond haired waitresses. We settled down to an enormous meal lubricated with beer and wine and further speculation about the possibility of setting up an emerald import export business using Fed Ex. The more we drank the more lucrative the business became.

ABANDONED IN THE TSODILO HILLS

We flew to the Tsodilo hills in Northern Botswana with Andrew who told us he had never flown there before. Judging by the apparent age of his face, I wouldn't have been surprised if he had told us that he had never flown anywhere before. As we approached the hills, he hit me in the shoulder and pointed to them. At first, I thought he was being helpful but then I realized that he was actually relieved. We landed on a typical dirt strip with nobody there, no sign of any life. Andrew took off, saying he would buzz the camp to let them know we had arrived. There was a brief interval, about 30 minutes, when we thought, hmm, what are we going to do if no one shows up? Fortunately, no sooner had this happy thought formed in our heat-baked brains than along came Victor in a converted ice cream van and whisked us away to the Hills. I didn't think to ask him how he came by the ice cream van. We were with Astrid and Gerry and Victor had set up two pup tents at the base of the Tsodilo Hills. The name Tsodilo in the original San language means, "sheer." The four hills rise in a rough line out of the shimmering desert of the Okavango Panhandle, their color changing according to the time of day. None of the hills is more than 1200 feet high but the way they rise from a flat terrain that stretches to the horizon as far as the eye can see creates a disproportionate sense of size and presence. The rocks were pink, gray, green, and home to many paintings, reminiscent of Lascaux, in France. The pictures showed rhino, lion, zebra, spiders, stylized wagon wheels, and some figures with huge erections, also seen in the Lascaux paintings. Astonishingly, based on the conclusions of many Ph. D. theses in anthropology, the latter are thought to represent the concepts of creation and growth. This astounding insight makes me feel much better about the value and quality of Ph. D. theses in anthropology. The physical body structure of Bushmen bears many similarities to that of the ancient Egyptians including an apron covering the female genitals and a permanent semi-erection amongst the men. To the San people the pictures are sacred—full of mystery, legend, and spiritual significance. The bulk of the paintings date from between 800—1300 AD and more than 3500 paintings have now been recorded. The San believe that the four hills (male, female, child and North) were where God first dropped his people and their cattle from the heavens. Since then the ancestors of the San have lived in the region leaving their stone tools, bone implements and, above all, the rock paintings.

When Laurens Van der Post first arrived in the 1950s his failure to sacrifice a warthog and a steenbok did not show sufficient respect for the "spirits of the hills." As a result his vehicles broke down, his cameras and tape recorders failed to function, he was attacked by a swarm of angry bees and his workmen abandoned the safari. Van der Post was so shaken that he buried a hand-written apology in a bottle beneath a panel of paintings that now bears his name. The spirits "accepted" his apology and allowed him to complete his journey without further mishap. Van der Post describes his experiences in his book "*The Lost World of the Kalahari.*"

Soon after we got to camp, Victor led us on a walk though the hills following the Leopard Trail. The hills are massive, emanating a mystique that comes from large rocks, especially those imbued with human spirituality as these were. We saw the paintings and marveled at their antiquity and the primal nature of Africa when they were painted before the taint of European settlement and the seeds of destruction of a way of life that was in harmony with the lands and nature. I should say that I am not some kind of anthropological Luddite, wishing things could have stayed as they were. The change was inevitable, however as Daniel Quinn wrote in his book *Ishmael*, the transition from leavers to takers is not one of *Homo sapiens'* finer moments. I often think that the best hope is to infuse technology as quickly as possible into developing communities. It is obvious and patronizing to point out that their culture and lifestyle is admirably fitted to their environment and that their culture is one that is self-sustaining. This is true but once a single idea from the "more developed" world finds its way into these cultures then the system is irreversibly broken. By the time we returned to camp, Victor's mate had made a superb meal and the four of us settled down to dine *al fresco* as night fell. As we looked back up into the hills, we could see forest fires burning. The fires burning on the Hills made them eerie and filled with foreboding. We sought to dispel the feeling with that most efficacious nostrum, gin.

The next morning we piled into the ice cream van and began a journey to a camp called Nxamaseri on the Okavango River. When we arrived a charming South African couple, Guy and his wife Beverly greeted us. The camp was the stuff of Africa. The rooms were tented over wooden floors with views of the Okavango River. We settled in and then repaired to the fire for gin and conversation. Upon returning to our tent to freshen up for dinner, we found our room totally upturned and bloody footprints all over the floor. Some vervet monkeys had mistaken a pack of antihistamine pills for sweets and had rampaged through our room. One of the little buggers had managed to cut his foot on a tin mosquito-repellent burner and had proceeded to bleed all over the place. This was the time when some scientists speculated that SIV could be the origin of HIV; consequently, a couple of pints of monkey blood were not what we wanted in our tent. As we made our way back to the bar, we heard a shot and found that Guy had had to shoot a spitting cobra that had taken up residence in a garden by the path and was trying his luck on the passers by.

Before supper, Guy took us out on the river for a pre-prandial cruise. No sooner had we left the dock than the river in front of us boiled up as a male hippo ran along the river bottom in front of the boat. This reminded us that we definitely didn't want to be in a mokoro with this guy around. As we talked that night, the prospect of fishing came up. Fishing is not my bag, I might have caught a few roach in the Cherwell as a kid, but fishing had rather passed me by, or was it the other way round? My tepid interest caused a distinct pall on Guy's demeanor and we quickly realized, or rather remembered, that this was a fishing camp! So we all gamely said we would love to go fishing. The prospect of sitting with a rod and line watching some float bobble when you are on the banks of one of the most romantic of African Rivers seemed incongruous, but hey, when in a Botswana fishing camp…The next day after breakfast we all piled into Guy's boat and off we went after tigers. As we motored down the river, we went under a tree on which was sitting an African Fish eagle. The eagle was about two feet tall with chocolate brown body and pure white head and bib feathers. A scimitar-like bright yellow beak and a piecing eye offset the stark head plumage. The eagle's eerie and haunting call is a hall mark of the delta. A little further along we passed a sandy rock face in which hundreds of carmine bee-eaters had built nests. These gorgeous birds have a turquoise head and a black eye band making them look ready to rob a bank. Their body is carmine red and the base of the tail flashes turquoise as they fly. They flashed and rolled above the river creating an exotic feel as we slipped by the papyrus reeds and soon encountered the first of many Nile crocodiles.

We began casting for tigers. Tiger fish are what your cousin from Alabama would call sport fish. Sport in the sense that it will happily bite your finger off; tiger in the sense that it is striped, has big teeth and fights like the devil. We had the chance to experience all three of these attributes first hand. We were busily and inexpertly casting when all of a sudden Gerry got a bite and landed an eighteen inch fish, Nancy then caught one, then Astrid, and then…no, alas, I did not. Gerry proceeded to demonstrate his virility and high testosterone levels by catching five fish. As we motored home, I managed to land the smallest Tiger fish caught that day. We were about to throw it back when Guy asked us to keep it. As we passed near the tree in which we had seen the fish eagle Guy held my minnow in his hand. The fish eagle flapped its wings, rose in the air, and then came head on at us, grasping the fish out of Guy's hand and soaring in the air back to its perch where it proceeded to tear the fish apart and devour it before our eyes.

As we drifted back down the Okavango to the distant cry of a fish eagle, we could see the heads of crocodiles, floating between air and water like old hard, knobbly, tree bark. Occasionally the crocs would turn in the water to reveal their soft, shiny, baby-puke green bellies. They stared at us with their jade-green eyes.

HEADLESS CROCODILE

The Okavango Delta in Botswana is one of the few inland Deltas in the world. It rises in Angola and flows southeast emptying its water into the Delta where it creates a flooded area of 6000 square miles to which many species of animal are drawn. The southern most point of the Great Rift is the Gumare fault. This fault which runs NE to SW forms a barrier that causes the Okavango basin to fan out to form the inland Delta. One of the many remarkable experiences in the delta is to come across herds of buffalo. Once they scent you the animals will fix you with their incomparable bank manager stare and then suddenly start running. The sound of several hundred Cape buffalo charging through the knee-deep water is like standing next to a freight train going over an iron bridge. Crocodiles laze in the tall grass and slip into the water without noise or ripple. It was here that we were riding. There is nothing quite so exciting as galloping through water, especially if the water has crocodiles in it not to mention that the grass provides perfect cover for lion.

The operators of this safari were PJ and Barney. PJ was born in Namibia and trained as a geologist. This took him to Botswana which he loved so much that he emigrated and became a Motswana citizen. He has a visceral dislike of snakes, in large part from having been bitten by a mamba and managing to survive. When I first encountered him, he rode into camp with a baby's disposable diaper wrapped around his knee. He had been bitten on the inside of his calf by some poisonous spider or other and the padding afforded by the diaper was the only way he could manage to ride. His wife Barney is a Brit, a notable horsewoman who at the age of eleven jockeyed the Arabian horses of the Arab Shiek, Bin Suman Al Kanifa, in the flat races staged in the deserts of Bahrain. I would say they are typical eccentric African horse safari operators. When we encountered them, they had one of a long line of delightful dogs. This one was a pit bull named Tubu. He was a little the worse for wear from baboon fights and this proved to be his demise as with so many of his predecessors.

One night as we sat around the fire, PJ asked if anyone would like to spend the night on the game platform. This was an improvised game viewing platform about 30' up a Sausage tree (*Kigelia pinnata*) overlooking a pond. The tree is so called because it has fruit that dangle from long stalks like giant sausages. They may be up to two feet long and weigh up to 15 pounds each.

We had ridden by the pond earlier and noted that it contained a headless crocodile. That is just the sort of thing you do when riding in Africa. You can imagine the scene, trotting along enjoying the sun and the bird song, perhaps sharing a pleasant aside with one's riding companions when, whoa, there's a headless crocodile in that pond. Crocodile heads are powerful juju. Juju is a West African word thought to be a corruption of the colonial French joujou meaning a toy or plaything. As the O. E. D. goes on to say, *"An object of any kind superstitiously venerated by West African native peoples, and used as a charm, amulet, or means of protection; a fetish. Also, the supernatural or magical power attributed to such objects, or the system of observances connected therewith.* In Africa every time a crocodile is killed, the local shamans will come and take the head. Quite what they do with it is unclear; although the story is that when dried and mixed with dried snake, it is a powerful poison (now there's a surprise). The power of these things should in no way be underestimated. Tristan Voorspuy tells the story of how on one safari some things were being stolen from the kitchen. Of the 25 or so staff, no one was willing to talk. Therefore, on the advice of the head syce he procured a piece of elephant tusk, buried it in the ground, and then asked each camp member to jump over the ivory and swear that he was not the thief. As his turn came, one man broke down and confessed that he was the villain rather than jump over the ivory. I recently came across an interesting reference to the use of ivory in Maasai culture that supports this story. Ol Lana, who was a legendary laibon or spiritual leader, had achieved fame as spokesman between the Maasai and the British at the turn of the century. Ol Lana's possessed a sacred ivory horn made from an elephant's tusk. If cursed through this horn the Maasai said you were as good as dead; if blessed, your good fortune was assured.

I volunteered to spend a night on the platform. Its funny to recall how easy that was to do when sitting around the campfire having quaffed a few beers with your fellow punters. That night, after I climbed up the rope ladder with my sleeping bag and what turned out to be a rather inadequate flash light, I did not feel quite so blasé. I convinced myself that lions could not climb trees but, on reflection, I realized that leopards could. Actually there are two places in East-Africa where lions do climb trees and stay there sometimes up to 7 hours. One is Lake Manyara in Northern Tanzania and the other is Ishasha in Uganda. Of course, I speculated that a pride in the Okavango, not a million miles from the headless crocodile-containing pond could also at that very time be contemplating a shin up the nearest Sausage tree, and what about snakes, don't a lot of them live in trees? Snakes with names like snouted night adder, black spitting cobra, and the much-feared black mamba. The mamba can deliver100 to 400 milligrams of venom in a bite, which is serious when you consider that the lethal dose for humans is 10 to 15. Mambas contribute to a lot of folklore in Africa. In part, this is because their venom is a neurotoxin that rapidly paralyses its victim but doesn't actually kill it. As a result people noted that black mamba victims often took several days to rot, simply because they weren't dead. Moreover, in some cases people simply got up and walked away after several days. Presumably, the latter could still breathe. Today, if a mamba bites you and the antivenin does not work the standard therapy is to put you on a heart lung machine and hope for the best, always assuming of course that your local bush cottage hospital has one to spare.

As I lay on the platform straining to hear animals approaching the pond, leaves started to fall off the damned sausage tree. For every leaf that fell my heart sped up slightly as I imagined a thick muscular python slowly winding its way down one of the branches towards me. This was not quite as fanciful as it might seem. One of the guides in PJ's camp, a fellow named Tirelo Xanekhwe, had just been telling me that very afternoon how he was walking back to camp and saw a python catch a baboon by the foot. It then proceeded to crush the baboon and swallow it whole.

I shone my feeble torch into the limbs above me, and seeing no snakes I promptly fell asleep until I was woken by PJ at 6 am having seen nothing but my own visions of snakes and leopards. The croc was still bobbing headless on the water as we drove past.

Persuading Your Pilot to Take All Your Stuff

We arrived at Maun airport from Victoria Falls with enough stuff to set up a M.A.S.H. Maun lies at the Southern fringes of the Okavango Delta and is a staging post for safaris going into the Delta. When we entered the arrivals hall at Maun airport, Neville met us. Neville was a type, young, handsome, and affecting an air of devil-may-care. Had he been born 50 years earlier he would doubtless have piloted a Spitfire in the Battle of Britain. Now, his source of excitement was ferrying people over Africa in small planes to vaguely defined landing strips in the middle of the bush. Neville took one look at our luggage and said you have to lose a bag. I have yet to meet a bush pilot who doesn't look at your luggage as if it were a pile of fresh dog feces. "Oh, no please, please our books," we whined. "Oh all right, bloody tourists." We flew to Xudum airport—i.e. a dirt strip in the Okavango Delta. Buzzed the strip to get rid of game and then bumped to a halt.

Flying to the Nyika Plateau

A few pages back I introduced you to Rank, the pilot who flew us from Chelinda to Lilongwe and then onto Windhoek. His counterpart who flew us from Lilongwe to Chelinda at the beginning of the trip was Russell. Russell, who is about 13 years old, turned up at Lilongwe airport in a Cessna 210 three hours late. He flew us up the center of Malawi at 9,500' to Chelinda, circled the rough looking grass runway to clear off any game that may have been lying on it and came in at a precarious angle—the altimeter read 8,500' at his approach and 7'500 when we hit the ground. We learned later this was a difficult strip and it was his first time! I had to admire his *sang-froid* in retrospect. As you may have gathered by now, nearly all the small plane flights I have taken in Africa seem to have involved some aspect of it being the first time for the respective pilots.

9

Poachers, Hunters and Dogs

We were riding on the Nyika Plateau in Malawi. A place made famous by Laurens van der Post's book "*Venture to the Interior.*" Nyika is a Kiswahili word for a type of thorn bush but also means "uninhabited" and I can certainly attest to this being the more apt definition. The rolling landscapes of the center of the 8000ft plateau look like whalebacks but the edges of this granite core are scarp-like especially where, in the northeast, it forms the edge of the Great Rift Valley. Actually, the Nyika plateau separates two of the major faults of the Rift valley system—Lake Malawi to the East and the Luangwa Valley of Zambia to the West. It was mid-August when we were there and cold, since we were in the Southern hemisphere. In 1985 a record low of -6.7°C was recorded. Suffice it to say, that we have never been so cold in Africa. Our first night under canvas was so frigid that I had to wrap my underpants around my head; actually, they looked pretty good, they may not have smelled so good, but they definitely had a certain edge. There was four of us (Nancy, Astrid, Gerry and me) plus our guide David and his wife. We woke to cups of hot tea and watched as the syces loaded up the packhorse. Keeping the pack balanced is very tricky. As soon as it sits evenly on the horse another forgotten item is added and whammo the pack slides off to one side, the horse jumps in the air, the syces shout and we watch with increasingly bemused expressions. This was our first, and to date, only experience with a packhorse in Africa. Interestingly it was also David's first, and because of this trip, I suspect his only experience with a packhorse in Africa. Eventually the syces managed to get the packhorse loaded and we set off.

We were going down a narrow elephant trail to spend the night in a remote riverbed inaccessible by the four-wheel drive support vehicles. I should say that the morning we headed out it was sleeting. We looked like those sad pictures of American Indians slumped over their horses riding out into the teeth of a blizzard. The elephant path had probably been used for millennia and formed part of a migratory route from Tanzania to Zambia. Elephants, when relocated to areas where elephants used to live in the past, will re-discern their ancestor's old tracks even though an elephant has not walked them for decades. How can this be? Surely no spoor remains and there can be no genetic imprint. I think they use topographical pattern recognition, which is genetically selected for by evolution. Perhaps a fold to the land and the smell of underground springs lead the elephant to prefer a particular route even though the floral topography of the route will have changed beyond recognition in 50 years.

We followed the track, as it wound down a valley. Elephant tusks had scored the sand stone in the track sides as they sought salt from the mineral rock. Occasionally we would come across their cannon ball sized dung with its partially digested fibers. Elephant are very inefficient extractors of nutrition. Some 50% of the vegetation an elephant eats is not digested. As a result, they consume 5% of their typical 3,000 Kg body weight every day, which contributes to the damage elephant can wreak on the countryside in terms of uprooted bush and knocked-down trees.

Our revelry in the flowers and birds was brought up short as we rounded a bend in the track to find the haunch of a freshly butchered eland strung to a wooden pole and lying in the dust of the track. Next to the meat was an axe. There was a heavy silence as the blood oozed from the meat. The horses looked intently at the thick bush surrounding the track. David got off his horse and picked up the bloody axe, wrapped it in some cloth and put it in is saddlebag. We rode on, feeling eyes staring at us from the bush. We were about a hundred miles from anywhere and if these poachers had had guns or felt particularly belligerent to a group of whites taking their meat we could well have become history.

Coming across the poached eland caused all kinds of thoughts and emotions, anger and frustration at the butchery of such a beautiful animal that we had, in part, come all this way to see. Then, the sadness and reality that Malawi is one of the poorest countries in the world and who were we to say that its people should not kill its animals for meat? Then the realization that if they kill all the game and burn the entire bush to help in their game hunting no tourists will come and valuable foreign currency will disappear as well as their own natural heritage. This is just a small example of the intractable problems of Africa.

This reminds me of another occasion when I underwent a profound change in my thinking. We were riding in Botswana in the Okavango Delta. The Okavango is relatively protected not only as a wildlife game reserve but also because of the tsetse fly. Because of the inhospitability to domestic animals, a lot of this area of Botswana consists of approved hunting reserves. Typically, the reserve consists of a large tract of land rented out by the government to a manager who charges wealthy hunters to come and shoot animals—$30,000 for a leopard. As we were riding through the hunting preserve, we stayed in one of the hunting camps on the Kiri river, for a night. Behind the tented camps was a charnel house used to render the animals after they had been shot.

Inside the charnel house, amidst a cloud of flies were stacks of skins, skulls, elephant tails, and all the sad trophies of "brave" men who came, saw and shot the wild life. My initial reaction was one of incredulity that anyone could actually a) want to kill a leopard and b) think him (her) self anything other than wretched for doing it. Yet, these people, who took only a very small fraction of the game, helped pay to preserve this huge tract of land for the rest of the animals and for us. So perhaps it was a win-win strategy (unless, of course you happen to be the leopard in the crosshairs). The managers of these reserves work very hard to curtail poachers simply because they have a huge financial interest in maintaining stocks of game. The problem with this model is that the vast majority of the money goes to corrupt officials and very little to locals who lose out twice, once because they cannot farm the land and secondly because they cannot hunt the game. At the end of the day, I must say, I support these reserves. I have seen what has happened in Kenya where population growth has resulted in the farming of poor soil that is fit only for wild bush and the animals that live in it. The natural flora and fauna of many African countries really has to be viewed much like diamonds, gold, or other natural resources and carefully husbanded and managed. The only way to do that is to provide the government and ideally the local people a financial incentive that outweighs other, perhaps easier, ways of exploiting the land. The key is making sure the local people benefit, both because it is a moral imperative since it is their land, but also as we have been discussing here, without that support poaching will finish off the game.

Horses are not allowed into the Maasai Mara, so after riding through the Loita Hills, crossing the Mara River (and dodging the odd bloat of hippos) and heading south to the Maasai Mara game park we camped in a bend in the Mara and boarded our supply Land Rover for a game drive in the park. There we were, about six of us perched on top of the Land Rover looking at the game grazing on the mesmerizing Mara plain. I believe pressures unique to this environment selected some of the properties of our brain. For example, perhaps this environment fixed in our genome the genes conferring the ability to look out over a plain and see potential campsites, water holes, or develop a successful hunting strategy. If you accept the precepts of this argument then it seems likely to me that we (by which I mean our brains) also have some affinity for these primordial topographies. Perhaps we feel safer, more at ease, in an environment that shaped our brains. We simply feel at home. Michael Pollan has advanced similar arguments for human's fondness of lawns. In his book *Second Nature,* Pollan argues that a well-manicured lawn, especially a park or one of those rolling continuous multi family lawns that are such a hallmark of suburban America, are surrogates for the savannah where man took his first step. The savannah offers an unobstructed view for sighting both predators and prey. This enabled the early humans that lived in them to survive, to breed, and to pass along those "grass-appreciation" genes that are now baked into our genomes (and support the $5bn lawn care industry in the US). As I said earlier, Nancy and I feel our love of Africa is a result of seeing the Maasai Mara and hearing that echo in our genomes bounce back into our minds.

Nevertheless, there we were watching some zebra and wildebeest munching on grass when all of a sudden the inestimable Mark threw the Land Rover into gear and hurtled off at top speed towards, what seemed to us at best, a few specks on the horizon. As we hung on for life, we closed on the scene. A Maasai dog was savaging a young Thompson's gazelle. The Maasai have a strange relationship with dogs. They consider them unclean and never touch them or feed them; as a result, they are almost feral. This particular dog was obviously intent on killing the Tommy. We pulled up and Mark drew his gun and shot the dog. This cast a pall over the Land Rover. There was something about a gun firing in the park that was very poignant.

Mark is, without doubt, a tough honcho.

Mark and Topper

On our very first safari in Kenya, we were heading into camp at the end of a long day's ride. It is invariably a time of peace and well-being. You are full with the day's experiences and pleasantly tired after the long ride and relieved that you have survived another day. The African evening cups the land in a gold light and you can taste the gin and tonic cutting through the red dust in your mouth. Suddenly Mark rode off full tilt through the thorn bushes in pursuit of a poacher. The latter was instantly recognizable by his dog, spear, and western garb. The poacher hurled his spear at Mark, incredibly Mark's horse leapt sideways and the spear narrowly missed Mark. Mark leapt from his horse and had a detailed physical conversation with the man. Later that night some Maasai from a nearby village came into our camp to ask about the event. Mark pointed out that we were here to see animals and we paid the Maasai a rent for camp and a bonus if we saw game. Clearly, this poacher was not conducive to this business arrangement. It is a disconcerting thing to see a white man beat a black man in a country like Kenya so freighted is this land with its colonial legacies. Mark tells many sad tales of elephants shot with poisoned arrows and then tracked for days as they die; of corrupt officials who have no interest in checking the destruction of game or environment. It is a sad tale, which I only make sadly familiar. I find myself from time to time lulled with the perspective of the long view. In earth's history, probably more than a billion species have evolved and disappeared. What are a few rhinos and lions compared to this? Why bother? Unless you believe in some overarching spiritual force, and even if you do then surely this force is also part of the evolutionary process—Darwin's Universal Acid. After all, technological evolution with the ensuing consumption, destruction, and pollution is all part of *Homo sapiens'* behavior, just as knocking down trees is for *Loxodanta Africana.* Whilst we're taking the long view, the upper limit on the lifetime of Earth is about 5 billion years. Therefore, we are roughly half way through its lifetime. In about 2.5 billion years, the sun will have used up its hydrogen reserves and will expand to become a Red Giant, with a radius of about Earth's orbital distance thus swallowing up the Earth. Well before that, the earth will probably get hit by a good sized meteorite which will in all likelihood finish off a lot of the animals we tend to focus on in terms of preserving them, including good old *Homo sapiens.*

Not all poaching we encountered was of game animals. We visited the island of Rubondo in Lake Victoria. It is a pristine wilderness famous for its sitatunga antelope and its water birds. Because the whole island is a national park, there is no fishing for a mile around its coast. Nancy and I chartered a small boat to take us to one of the islands off Rubondo, imaginatively named Bird Island. We were intent on seeing nesting open billed stork and African fish eagles. As we approached the island, our captain pointed out some locals who were poaching fish. We sped over to find them hauling in gill nets filled with tilapia. Normally the game wardens impound the boats of poachers, tow them to Rubondo, and burn them. Luckily, for these chaps the warden was taking us to Bird Island so he gave them a talking to and we snagged a half dozen of their fish, not a very noble or effective punishment I suspect. Indeed, at the end of it, I think we were poachers ourselves. All in all its rather a sad business as these men were clearly fishing to feed their families and living on almost nothing, and yet if the waters are fished out the birds will disappear and so will the tourists and their dollars. Of course, the men hauling in the gill nets could care less about tourists. After all, they are the reason that they cannot fish the tilapia with impunity. It doesn't take long before this argument becomes similar to those put forward by both sides in the cod fisheries of New England.

In spite of all this, we returned to our camp to find all the rangers were fishing for tilapia off the shore. They used the most primitive equipment consisting of a piece of split bamboo with about 10 feet of line attached. The hook is baited with filamentous green algae picked off the rocks. We tried our hand, and no sooner had we cast the algae laden hook into the water than we hooked a tilapia and then another. The only difference was that we were fishing for fun; they were fishing for their supper.

10

Exploring the Rift

"The devil drives"

—*Richard Francis Burton*

The Great Rift Valley features strongly in many of our rides. The Rift is a vast geological and geographical feature of East Africa created by the separation of the African and Arabian tectonic plates around 35 million years ago. It runs from northern Syria to central Mozambique, a distance of 5,000 km, although it also exerts influence in Northern Botswana with geological faults controlling the location of the Okavango Delta. As I mentioned before the southern most point of the Great Rift is the Gumare fault that caused the Okavango basin to fan out to form the Delta. The true Rift Valley varies in width from 30-100 km and in depth from a few hundred to several thousand meters.

In eastern Africa, the Rift divides into two, the Eastern or Kenya Rift and the Western Rift. Some of the highest mountains in Africa form the edge of the western Rift, including the Ruwenzori Range or the Mountains of the Moon, thought by Ptolemy to be the source of the Nile. It also contains the Rift Valley lakes, which include the deepest lakes in the world such as the 1,470 meters deep Lake Tanganyika. Lake Victoria, the second largest freshwater lake in the world, is part of the Rift Valley system although it actually lies between the two branches. The Eastern Rift, or main section of the valley, cuts across Ethiopia and then south across Kenya, Tanzania, and Malawi to Mozambique. Lake Malawi lies in the Eastern Rift branch.

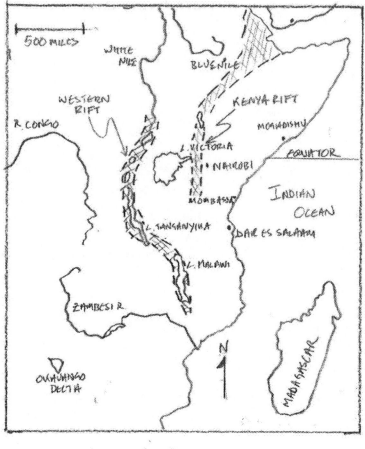

RIFT VALLEYS

Rift Valleys

The original faulting activity that created the Rift weakened the Earth's crust along its margins. The area is therefore volcanically and seismically active and has produced the volcanic mountains of, Mount Karisimbi, Mount Nyiragongo, Mount Meru and Mount Elgon as well as the Crater Highlands in Tanzania. The formation of the Rift Valley continues today and within a few million years, eastern Africa will probably split off to form a new landmass. I like to remember that the tectonic plates are still moving. If you take the long view the whole of earth's current crust or mantle will eventually be taken down into the molten core of the earth and be replaced by "new" material. Thus all of man's pollution, artifacts, lumps of plutonium and plastic bags will all go down into the melting pot and be purified by the cauterizing fire. Those of you out there who despair of what man is doing to the planet can perhaps take some solace from this and hope that we do not master the skill of interstellar travel so that we can carry our polluting habits to other parts of the Universe. Having written this little diatribe I must remind myself that all of the "pollution" that man has wrought is really only a consequence of Darwinian evolution and therefore is perfectly "natural" and thus must be in synchrony with the fundamental laws of nature and Darwin's universal theory. If you can accept this then perhaps the only thing to do with one's life is to try to make as many organisms as possible happy or at least to reduce their physical and intellectual suffering while they are on earth.

The Rift Valley has been a rich source of anthropological discovery, especially in Olduvai Gorge. The rapidly eroding highlands have filled the valley with sediments, thus creating a favorable environment for the preservation of remains. The bones of several hominid ancestors of modern humans have been found there, including those of "Lucy", a nearly complete australopithecine skeleton, which was discovered by anthropologist Donald Johanson. In addition, Richard and Maeve Leakey who have done so much significant work in this region, and indeed so much to promote wildlife in Kenya, have made the region most famous.

Subterranean movement is common today as the Rift Valley is home to thirty active and semi-active volcanoes and countless hot springs along its length. This string of alkaline lakes and boiling springs northwest of Nairobi includes Lake Baringo, Lake Bogoria, Lake Nakuru, Lake Elementaita, Lake Naivasha, and Lake Magadi in the south. These lakes are unique because their water contains a high concentration of sodium carbonate due to the high alkalinity from the surrounding volcanic rocks coupled with poor drainage outlets because of the steep sides of the valley. The high evaporation of the surface lake water results in the formation sodium carbonate that, in turn, creates an ideal breeding ground for algae. Several species of fish, tilapia in particular, thrive in this environment. As a result, millions of birds flock to these soda lakes to feast on the abundant food supply of algae and fish. Each of the lakes in the Rift Valley string has a slightly different water composition ranging from freshwater to extremely alkaline, highly saline to brackish. One of the most remarkable sites is the huge flocks of lesser flamingos drawn to the alkaline waters. Flamingos filter blue-green algae called Spirulina from these waters and in so doing gain the pigment that gives them their wonderful color. I remember well visiting Lake Niavasha and standing in thrall on its shores as tens of thousands of flamingos waded and fed in the water not 10 yards from me.

LAKE TANGANYIKA

The first non-Africans to see Lake Tanganyika were Richard Burton and John Speke in February 1858. Burton was an adventurer par excellence, being the first Caucasian to enter the city of Harrar in the Sudan and one of the first non-Moslems to gain access into Mecca, which he did disguised as a Pathan merchant. Here is how Bram Stoker, of Dracula fame, describes his meeting with Burton. *The man riveted my attention. He was dark, and forceful, and masterful and ruthless. I have never seen so iron a countenance…I never saw anyone like him. He is steel and would go through you like a sword. Burton's face seemed to lengthen when he laughed; the upper lip rising instinctively and showing the right canine tooth…As he spoke the upper lip rose and his canine tooth showed its full length like the gleam of a dagger.* This description has raised speculation that Burton may be the model for Stoker's Dracula. Burton traveled the world in the 1850's and 60's when the going was a little tougher than it is today. On top of his travel exploits, he also could speak 29 languages; he translated the Kama Sutra and Perfumed Garden into English, and was an expert swordsman. As I rode through Africa I often thought of him and his peers walking over the same country one hundred and fifty years earlier in search of a river or a lake, without maps or medicine. For many of his contemporaries the drive was colonial expansion and the attendant riches or some sense of spiritual superiority that found expression through conversion of the Africans to Christianity. I think that Burton's motive was to put himself on his particular edge and for someone of his courage and intellect this edge involved some very dangerous journeys. Burton and Speke had started out from Kaole (now ruined but near the coastal town of Bagamoyo on the Tanzanian coast opposite Zanzibar) and walked west in search of the source of the Nile. Their route took them a distance of 955 miles, which they covered in seven and a half months. They found Lake Tanganyika, however, Burton quickly realized that it was not the source of the Nile because it had no major river flowing out of it. Nevertheless, he does express his joy in his writings at finding this beautiful freshwater lake having endured untold hardships on the journey from Kaole. Here is the passage from his book *The Lake Regions of Central Africa*, in which he describes first seeing the lake: "*Nothing in sooth could be more picturesque than this first view of the Tangany-*

ika lake, as it lay in the lap of the mountains, basking in the gorgeous tropical sun-shine." By a cruel twist of fate the real source of the Nile, the Victoria Nyanza was found on their return trip by Speke and resulted in a very controversial public argument between the two explorers as to whether it was the real source of the Nile.

I have swum in Lake Tanganyika and can attest to the beauty and gin-clarity of its waters. I remember gulping down the water and imagining what it must have been like for Burton to come across the lake. It was an uncanny experience because the lake is so big my brain kept telling me it must be the sea and not to drink it. Here is how Burton describes the taste: "*The water of Tanganyika appears deliciously sweet after the salt and bitter, the putrid and slimy produce of the wells, pits and pools of the line of march.*" (Burton *ibid*).

Burton and Speke reached Lake Tanganyika at what is still called Ujiji. This town has earned its place in history for being the site where Stanley met Livingstone in 1871, and there is a granite memorial to commemorate the event.

We first arrived at Lake Tanganyika in a small plane, not to join a horse safari but as part of a walking safari through northern Tanzania. We landed at Lagossa, which is some 100 miles south of Ujiji on the shores of the lake and boarded a boat that was to ferry us to Mahale. The boat was made from rough-hewn planks of wood lap straked to create a large dory. The captain was a delightful, if taciturn fellow with a fez and a caftan that billowed in the breeze set up by the 150 h.p. out board motor. Mahale is a chimp preserve on the east shore of Lake Tanganyika some 200 miles south of Gombe, the preserve made famous by Jane Goodall. Toshisada Nishida first researched the chimps of Mahale. Over the years, one unit of chimps has become acclimated to humans. This gave us the opportunity to walk into the forest and encounter them in their natural habitat. We entered the forest along rough, narrow trails overhung with vines and all manner of equatorial trees. The Kungwe Mountain loomed as a backdrop and every now and then, the tree canopy shook as black and white colobus or red tailed colobus monkeys stretched to get a view of us. Suddenly, we rounded a bend in the track and there right in front of us on the trail were a dozen chimps. We crouched down and sat on the floor, no more than ten feet away. They seemed completely oblivious to us and we were careful to avoid eye contact and generally adopted a very passive demeanor. As we sat with them, they sprawled on the ground, picked nits from each other's coats and seemed very relaxed. Young chimps wrestled and played with each other, running up and down the trees and swinging from thin branches with one hand. I watched one mother with her small baby as he swung from her back onto a branch. She immediately reached up and placed her hand over his as if to ensure he didn't lose his grip. Suddenly, for no apparent reason, this tranquil scene was shattered by all the chimps starting to scream and hoot. They climbed up trees and beat the branches and then, just as quickly, everything went quiet and they resumed their former calm.

A story appeared in the paper recently describing a couple in the States who owned a chimp as a pet. As they grew older, they put the chimp in a sanctuary with other chimps. They went to visit it and suddenly two other chimps attacked the man, tore off his face, ripped off his testicles, and bit off one of his feet. After reading the story I reflected back on how we sat within three feet of a troop of chimps who could very well have decided that they had had enough of these damn *homo sapiens* coming into their territory and sitting where they liked. After all, do we think that having a bigger frontal cortex gives us the right to simply squat in their forest? Well we'll show 'em who is boss in this neck of the woods. Fortunately, that didn't happen, although I have heard reports that Jane Goodall can no longer walk through Gombe because the chimps will attack her.

Mahale is one of the most remote and beautiful preserves in the world. Our camp was on the white sand beach with the forest behind us. In the middle of the night, I awoke to a deep thrumming sound coming off the lake. I went to investigate and on the horizon, I could see the lights of a freighter churning its way North. I discovered that the freighter was the Liemba. The Germans assembled it in 1913 in Kigoma after having transported it by rail from Dar es Salaam. During the First World War, the Germans dominated Lake Tanganyika with three war ships. A white hunter named John Lee, suggested that the British government send two gun ships to Cape Town, then by rail to the Congo and then drag them through the Congo and launch them on Lake Tanganyika, thereby surprising the Germans and wresting back control of the Lake. Incredibly, the Brits undertook this hare-brained scheme under the command of a character named Geoffrey Spicer-Simson. Spicer, as he was called, was rather colorful. Tattoos of snakes and butterflies covered his body and he would appear sporting a khaki skirt. When his men looked askance at his skirt he replied, "I designed it myself. My wife makes 'em for me. Very practical for the hot weather." He had wanted to call the two gunboats "Cat" and "Dog" but the Admiralty refused so he settled with Mimi and Toutou. He managed to get the boats to the lake and to sink one of the German ships. Belgian planes sank one of the others but the last one, the Graf von Götzen, survived.

In 1916, as Germany lost control of the lake they decided to scuttle the von Götzen off the entrance to the Malagarassi River, having first carefully greased all her working parts to prevent corrosion. After the war, the Belgians raised her but she sank near the entrance to Kigoma. This whole adventure was widely reported. Indeed the British success was the basis for C. S. Forester's novel *The African Queen.* Clearly, it reached Churchill's ears such that when he became First Lord of the Admiralty again, in 1921, he ordered the Götzen refloated. In 1924, the British Railway Administration recovered her. The quality German engineering coupled with the purity of the lake's water resulted in the von Götzen steaming again on Monday May 16 1927. She was put back in service as *Liemba,* the Kirungu word for "lake." Since then, the Liemba has steamed the lake from end to end almost continuously, for a period of 85 years. Estimates are that she has steamed over 4 million kilometers and is the oldest operational passenger vessel in the world. In 1993, the Liemba was refitted with diesel engines, and it is these that signaled her presence to me in Mahale.

Chimps have an interesting social structure. There is a dominant male, however females in estrus will mate with several different males. Because of this, chimps have evolved large testicles, presumably because their sperm has to compete with that of other males for any particular female's ovum. One way to compete is to increase the volume of the ejaculate. Gorillas on the other hand have a harem structure in which the dominant male wins a harem and keeps other males out. As a result, female gorillas in estrus do not mate with other gorillas and the dominant male has no need to compete at the semen level. Evidence for this comes from the relatively small size of a gorilla's testicles. He does, however, have to threaten and intimidate other males when they move into his territory. This need has selected for strong sexual dimorphism in gorillas with the males becoming much larger than the females. It has probably occurred to you by now that if the forgoing logic is true then one may be able to infer something about a primate's social structure by measuring the size of the male's testicles relative to its body weight, and you'd be right. Harvey and Pagel have combed the literature and plotted the body size versus testicle size for many primates. Those species that lie below the line, i.e. that have smaller testicles than their body size might suggest, tend towards a harem structure and those above the line do not. Where is *Homo sapiens* you may ask? Well, we tend to lie slightly below the line. This may gain thin support from the observation that many human cultures have seen polygamy and harems, indeed the Mormons practice such behavior to this day.

We can learn a great deal about humans by studying our fellow primates. For example, take this observation. The relationship between the mean number of individuals with whom an animal can maintain social relationships by personal contact (N), and the ratio of neocortical volume (essentially the frontal cortex of the brain) to the volume of the rest of the brain (CR), is shown for 36 primate genera by the following equation:

$$\text{Log (N)} = 0.093 + 3.389 \log \text{(CR)}$$

When one plugs in the CR for *Homo sapiens* the predicted group size is 147.8 (95% confidence limits are 100.2—231.1).

The discoverer of this relationship is Robin Dunbar. He went on to calculate how much time primates spend grooming in these social groups and found that chimpanzees, which have the next highest CR after humans, spent 20% of their time grooming. By extrapolation, humans would have to spend 42% of their time grooming. This would place an extraordinary burden on the species, therefore Dunbar hypothesized that, as an evolutionary response, we developed language to take the place of grooming. Interestingly, when left to our own devices, most human conversational groups consist of four people, which restores the "grooming time" to chimpanzee levels or less.

Following discovery of the number 147.8, Dunbar searched for data that measured natural human groupings. Here are some of the interesting things he found:

- The average size for hunter-gatherer societies is 148.4 (range 90-221.5; N=9)

- The size of Neolithic Mesopotamian villages suggests 150-200 inhabitants.

- Most armies have a basic unit of 150 people. The Roman maniple was 130 men. The company in modern armies is invariably 100-200 strong.

- The Hutterites regard 150 people as the maximum number for their farming communities, once it reaches that size it is split into two.

- Gore-tex manufacturing plants are limited to 150 people. "A lattice organization operates most effectively", Gore said, "when plants are kept to a size of no more than 150 associates." The firm's founder, who died in 1986, believed that people who know one another work better together.

Thus, several different data sets come up with the same number predicted by Dunbar's equation. One reason for the existence of this number could be because our brains can only handle interacting with a small number of people and we feel and function better in groups of this size. As group size increases, for example in large corporations, we find complex systems are required to keep everyone in check and unproductive behaviors begin to emerge. This would be equally true as we moved from small rural villages into towns and cities.

On the other hand, people in smaller groups find it easier to live up to the expectations of their peers with whom they often have a personal relationship. Within a corporate setting, peer pressure is often a much more powerful motivator than a boss and at-risk financial rewards, which are often experienced in a negative way.

As I reflected on this argument, I wondered if the "new information age" would change the number in the same way that the evolution of language enabled proto-*Homo sapiens* to expand its social group size to 150. Does email, the telephone, or video conferencing do the same? I do not have any data, but I do have a hunch and the answer is no. My reasoning is that when you talk to people and gossip with them you exert peer pressure, raise expectations, and develop unwritten contracts and exhibit all the complex human behaviors that have recently been subsumed under the abbreviation "EQ"—emotional quotient (*Daniel Goleman*). It is these qualities that create exceptional performance within companies, as indicated in a recent analysis by Collins. He found that leaders with high EQs appreciate the theory of the mind (the understanding of the minds of ourselves and others) and are the most successful in delivering high business performance.

However, it is very difficult to take advantage of a high EQ in large groups where the phone and email become the principal modes of communication (a.k.a. grooming) especially if you have never met, or seldom see, the person or group at the other end. This presents a challenge in large corporate environments, where the attraction of leveraging scale-driven cost savings can result in a loss both both of personal leadership and a feeling of connection.

Thanks to Dunbar, I think business, indeed all forms of human society today, could benefit from this piece of scientific observation and begin to reap the benefit of our minds by structuring our social and business groups with chimpanzees in mind.

LAKE EYASI

Lake Eyasi is another of the several lakes in the floor of the East African Rift Valley. It is located in northern Tanzania and the southwest flank of the famous Ngorongoro Volcano drains into the northeast end of the lake. Because of the low rainfall in the area the seasonal water level fluctuations in the lake are dramatic. Indeed, during years of low rainfall the lake evaporates to a dry soda crust. It was in just such a year that a group of us were driving to the foot of the 800m high Oldonyo Ibor escarpment which forms the Western shore of Lake Eyasi when we saw what looked like elephant tracks heading out into the dry lake bed. We decided to stop and look. A few of us walked out onto the bed and started to follow the tracks. This was an odd thing to do when we clearly couldn't see any elephants. I think we wanted to see why they were walking on the lakebed and how far they had gone, perhaps looking for water. I was behind the main group and was for some reason scanning around with my binoculars. I saw a white shape and knew immediately that it was a skull. It was about 500 yards away but I knew what it was, something pulled me towards it. I started to walk and the dry salty crust of the parched lakebed cracked under my feet. I could hear the rest of the group as they followed the elephant tracks. The heat was hard and the wind was blowing a fine dust into my face. After a couple of hundred yards, I saw part of a flamingo's wing lying on the ground in front of me. It must have been a juvenile because the feathers were speckled brown and white and where it attached to the body was still bloody. I picked it up and had the eerie sensation of feeling this soft warm wing, as if it were still attached to the bird. There were no other parts or feathers nor spoor around and it may have blown there from the site where it was killed.

I lifted my binoculars again and brought the white sphere into focus, yes, there was no doubt now, it was a primate skull, a big one. I walked on and with each step I could feel anticipation mingled with fascination that the skull was human. When I reached it, I could see that it was human. I looked around. There were no other bones but there were tracks of some animal, perhaps a hyena that had sunk into the slightly moist lakebed around the skull. I could imagine it sniffing the skull, checking it out, and then realizing there was nothing in it for him. The skull was lying on its side, sunk about half an inch into the dry mud. The water had obviously dried around it, leaving it to settle in its current place. Part of me wanted to pick it up, the other part of me felt that would be disrespectful.

My companions on that Tanganyika safari and I had spent a lot of time talking about spirituality. I am trained as a scientist and my first instinct is to deconstruct everything, to rationalize and to explain. I remember saying to a dear friend, what if we were sitting here 100,000 years ago as proto humans and looking at a thunderstorm, what would we make of the roiling clouds, the clash of thunder and the shrieks of lightening? Wouldn't we believe there was some life force above us that wasn't happy? Wouldn't we want to propitiate it, appease it, and do something to take away the physical fear and dread? That's how spiritual belief is born. However, the nature of that spiritual belief changes with time. As each century goes by, we understand more of the physical world. Today we can parse every aspect of a thunderstorm, deconstruct it to basic physics, and even deconstruct the emotion we feel about it. Couldn't many of our spiritual beliefs today be the result of a failure to understand the rational forces at work? The things to which we so readily assign spiritual origins such as the sense when a loved one dies thousands of miles away, the ability to anticipate a lover's word, the affirming beauty of sunsets, are these incarnations of some external spirit or are they mannequins upon which we lay our internal mysteries? On the other hand, is it that we just don't know enough of the rationale world to be able to explain them?

Whenever I fall into such a conversation, I find people become very emotional or condescending about the possibility that all spiritual phenomena are really a failure to understand the physical world. Sometimes I feel they are afraid, afraid that there may be nothing else, this is it, we are just another punctuation mark on the evolutionary thread, neither more nor less important than any other because there is no one to make that assessment, we simply are. Love is no less important, beautiful, or remarkable because it may someday be disaggregated and explained as an emergent phenomenon of various neuronal circuits that in turn have been laid down or modified by a life time's experiences. Therefore, when it is all said and done the minimalist hypothesis is that we simply don't understand enough at this dawn of the 21st century. Rather than open ourselves to the frightening (is it really that frightening?) possibility that we are no more than a bag of chemicals subject to some understood and some yet to be discovered laws, we invoke all manner of spiritual beliefs. If so, we have two choices, 'fess up and say we are scared or disappointed, or hold out the hope there is something bigger and that we will all be all right in the end because some thing somewhere has a purpose for all this. I think Shakespeare asked us to consider the same question in *Hamlet*. Act III, Scene 1:

To die; to sleep;

No more; and by a sleep to say we end

The heart-ache and the thousand natural shocks

That flesh is heir to. 'Tis a consummation

Devoutly to be wish'd. To die; to sleep

Of course, he immediately echoes the fears of all humankind by raising the specter that this is not all there is, that there is something still to come and "...*For in that sleep of death* what dreams may come?" and so spirituality or spiritual belief reasserts itself in the face of the last truly unanswerable question, what after death?

In spite of all these discussions, here I was in front of a skull hesitating to pick it up because, why? Because I felt her presence (I was sure it was a woman' skull), because I felt it would somehow be disrespectful. But wait a moment, she was dead, gone, if there is a soul or spirit it was not in this piece of dry bone.

Kamaria's skull

I bent down and looked at her closely, there was a small crack on the orbital surface, maybe the result of a blow? Apart from that, the skull was in perfect condition. Her teeth were smooth and perfect, I am no bone expert, but I guessed she was in her late twenties. And this is how she came to be there.…

Kamaria walked along the bush track just outside her village. It was night, a deep, yielding, African night with the Milky Way swirling across the sky. There were soft cries of babies and sounds of cooking in the village and farther off in the distance, the whup, whup of a hyena. She thought of Jafari. He was a handsome man, no doubt; he was mischievous and funny and he had a job, what more could she want? There was something missing, she knew it, and she knew it deep inside her heart. Her body didn't yearn for Jafari, she didn't want to stroke his thighs, she didn't want to taste his skin on her tongue, and she didn't want to feel his powerful body inside hers. She didn't feel that salty sensation in her mouth when she thought of him. Indeed, she never thought of him unless she forced herself to as she was now. No, all these feelings she could describe, and whose absence she could hold herself to account for, came to her when she thought of Lakeisha. Lakeisha, the name rolled on her tongue, she could taste her, she could feel her breasts tight against her own, she could look into her eyes and see her own soul. Lakeisha was her mundunugu, her siren. She had power over her. Lakeisha had only to put her hand on Kamaria's breast and she shuddered with passion, waves would roll through her body, she felt collected by Lakeisha's touch.

Kamaria gazed at the moon's reflection in the lake. Her name means "like the moon" and ever since she could remember moonlight created a calm within her, a fealty, a feral link. And tonight as she gazed into the lake at the moon's reflection, she determined to tell Jafari about Lakeisha.

Jafari pushed the boat out into the water. It was his father's boat, about 12 feet long and filled with nets and floats. To a Western eye, the boat looked like a New England dory. How the design reached Tanzania or whether the local fishermen invented it is lost in the past. Jafari was quiet and dignified as he paddled the boat out into the lake. He looked back at the village and could see the small flicker of flames from the cooking fires, but what attracted him was the great vast blackness around him. Why do people always focus on the light he wondered, when there is all that mystery and magic in the darkness? He paddled hard for about an hour until he was well into the middle of the lake. He looked calm, assuming the dignity of work, a man complete unto himself, a man. He reached down into the bottom of the boat and pulled up the sack. He opened it and took out Kamaria's head. Her hair was braided and fell around her cheeks and severed neck. Jafari dropped her head into the lake. The ripples disturbed the reflec-

tion of the moon, as he stared into the water Kamaria's head seemed to settle on the surface of the reflected moon.

11

I Never Thought I Would Die in Africa

A journey is like marriage. The certain way to be wrong is to think you control it.

—John Steinbeck Travels With Charley: In Search of America.

I did die in Africa, or at least that person who came there in 1996 died. I am not that man. Of course none of us stay the same, we all change. I was fortunate that my experience gave me a chance to look at my life, decide what was important and to seize the opportunity given to me by my illness and ensuing recovery to make some real changes in my life.

I remember well Dr. Patel telling me in Nairobi that it would take a year for me to recover fully. At the time that seemed crazy. My biggest concern was that some irreversible damage had been done to my lungs and that I would never recover. However, the lungs are remarkable both in their self-restorative capacity and in the slowness with which they do it.

After returning to Connecticut, I spent a month recuperating at home. I devoted a lot of time to thinking about my job and my life. I was so profoundly tired, but I do not think this was just the tiredness of a body that had been through it, I think the prospect of picking up my former life was exhausting. I am a scientist by training and started my career as a bench biochemist trying to discover new drugs. I moved to the managerial ladder and rose in those ranks until I found myself leading a department. However, as I matured I realized that I was an outsider. I had joined a big company seeking institutional love and of course never found it. I was anti-authoritarian to the bone and spent most of my time challenging the status quo and the institutional authority. Eventually I found a job as a strategist. The way I realized the role was to determine the future of health care and the role drugs would play in that future and then to try to kick my colleagues into preparing for that future. This was a hopeless task made doubly heavy by being self-inflicted. As I lay in bed trying to breath I felt it squat on my chest like an incubus.

All the self-help books, all the coaches, and all the king's analysts have but one piece of advice to offer and that is, to follow your heart. Do what makes you happy and damn the money, damn what your friends, lovers, or parents say, follow your heart. There is one other piece of wisdom I would like to add to this.

Some years ago, I took up bookbinding. I love books. I love their smell, feel, character, color, I love everything about them, and as I collected old books, I became interested in restoring them as they fell apart at the hinges or lost pages. To this end, I found a master. His name is Dan Knowlton and he lives in Bristol, Rhode Island. He is a dashing fellow of some eighty years. He is able to transform a moth eaten book into a worthy member of the most beautiful library. To which he adds the ability to encourage others and impart his skills with ease and affection. For two years, I went once a week to his small work shop and tried to learn some of the basic book binding skills. On the wall of his shop was a sign and this is what it said:

It is as follows:

Nothing in the world can take the
place of persistence.
Talent will not, nothing is more
common than unsuccessful people with
talent.
Genius will not; unrewarded genius
is almost a proverb.
Education will not, the world is full
of educated derelicts.

Persistence and determination alone are omnipotent.

It was not ascribed to anyone; it was only later that I found out that Calvin Coolidge said it in 1872. Of course Winston Churchill was a little more succinct when he said, "Never, never, never quit." But this kind of resolve comes only with limited vision and pig headedness or identifying your passion, that one thing that makes you happy, then you can really give it the Churchill treatment.

Therefore, you have to follow your heart with persistence and determination. If you can't persist you are not following your heart, if you are not following your heart you cannot persist, isn't life simple?

I quit my job. This was a real break with 23 years of friends and colleagues and a way of life and for me, perhaps most importantly, a family. I realize now that I joined a large company in search of a family, someone to love me and care for me. Of course, this is not what companies can or care to do. So, from the beginning I was expecting too much and always being disappointed. As soon as I really came to grips with this and let it go, a cold, wet woolen blanket fell from my shoulders. I immediately built a fire pit in my garden, started writing poetry and this book. I now choose various consulting jobs because they appeal to me and because people really want my help and advice. There is a tremendous charge to be working on things you enjoy, in places where you want to be and with people whom you like. I am a lucky man. Nearly dying in Africa gave me life.

Glossary

Acacia. This is a genus of trees first described by Linnaeus from Africa in 1773. They have spiny leaves and are often seen in the open savannah.

Afrikaans. Literally Dutch for African, this language is derived from Dutch but has borrowed many words from English, Portuguese and various African languages. It is one of the 11 official languages of South Africa. Ironically because of its dominance during apartheid it is widely used even between non-white Afrikaans as a lingua franca. Currently there are about 6 million Afrikaans speakers. The first book to be printed in Afrikaans was an Islamic religious text in 1856.

Benguela current. This current originates in Antarctica and flows north long the West Coast of Africa as far as southern Angola. It is responsible for the meteorological conditions that prevail in coastal Namibia giving rise to the Namib Desert among other phenomena.

Biltong. Strip of lean meat. Usually antelope or buffalo that has been dried in the sun. The name derives from the Afrikaans for buttock and tongue, because it is mostly cut from the buttocks.

Boerperd. A breed of horse first developed in the Cape after the Duct arrival in the latter half of 17th century. It has undergone many changes and crosses.

Comfrey. The common name of *Symphytum officinale*, long used for healing wounds. Here is a brief extract from Nicholas Culpepper's entry under Comfrey from his book entitled, "The English Physician Enlarged with three hundred and sixty nine medicines made of English herbs." published in 1792: "…The roots being outwardly applied, help fresh wounds or cuts immediately, being bruised and laid thereto; and is special good for ruptures and broken bones; yea, it is said to be so powerful to consolidate and knit together, that if they be boiled with dissevered pieces of flesh in a pot it will join them together again." No wonder Hanaliese put it on the horses' legs!

Dressage. The training of a horse in obedience and deportment. Derived from the French word meaning to train.

Engai. The Maasai's chief god, the sky-god. They believe that Engai gave them all the cattle in the world.

Enkang. A circle of huts, one per family, enclosed by a circular fence of thorn bushes. The woman of each household constructs the hut from cattle dung and clay. Periodically, the group will abandon their enkang and construct a new one in an area with better water and grazing.

Eukaryote. A life form made up of one or more eukaryotic cells. Eukaryotic cells are distinguished from the other major life form, the prokaryotes, in having a membrane surrounded nucleus that contains its DNA and organelles. Eukaryotes appear to have developed by the endocytosis of one prokaryote by another some 1.5 billion years ago.

Yellow Fever trees. Acacia xanthophloea. A member of the acacia family it has lime-green bark coated in a yellow powdery substance. It often has a flat crown and is favored as a nesting site. It obtained its name because it often grows in wet or marshy riverine woodlands and was associated with fever before it was realized that the mosquitoes, also found in these locations, were the vector.

Flying Doctor. The Flying Doctors started in 1957 as the East African Flying Doctor Service and is now known as AMREF (The African Medical Research and Education Foundation). Ironically, Nancy is on the American board of AMREF.

Genome. An organism's genetic material.

Herero. The Herero are a people belonging to the Bantu group of about 120.000 today. The majority among them lives in Namibia, whereas some live in Botswana or Angola. A subgroup among them is known as the Himba.

Kalahari. c.100,000 sq mi (259,000 sq km), in Botswana, Namibia, and South Africa. The Kalahari, covered largely by reddish sand, lies between the Orange and Zambezi rivers and is studded with dry lake beds.

Kiswahili. The word means coastal language and comes from the Arabic *sawahil* meaning coasts. It is a Bantu language that was heavily influenced by Arabs as they traded up and down the east coast of Africa at the turn of the first millennium. It is the *lingua franca* of well over 40 million people and is the national language of Tanzania.

Kopje. A small rocky outcrop derived from the diminutive of kop, Dutch for head.

Maa. A Nilo-Saharan language of the Maasai, Samburu and Camus peoples.

Maasai. The Maasai probably migrated from the Nile region of Sudan to central south-western Kenya and northern Tanzania around 1500 C.E. They are ai-pastoral peopl whose life and economy are centered around their cattle.
Makoro

Manyata. A Maasai homestead consisting of huts made of bent branches daubed with dried mud and cow-dung surrounded by a thorn fence, with separate huts for the father, each wife and her young children, and for the morans (warriors).

Mundunugu. East African witch doctor.

Ndau. A dialect of Shona. There are 1.5 million Ndau speakers in Eastern Zimbabwe and central Mozambique.

Prokaryote. Cell or organism lacking a membrane-bound, structurally discrete nucleus and other subcellular compartments.

Rooinek. Afrikaans for redneck used as a pejorative for Brits.

San. Khosian people of SW Africa (Botswana, South Africa, Namibia, and Angola), consisting of several groups and numbering about 110,000 in all. San is the name used for themselves. The apartheid whites in South Africa used to call the San bushmen.

Schutztruppe. Colonial armed force of Imperial Germany, disbanded at the end of the First World War in 1918.

Shuka. A long piece of fabric, commonly worn as a shawl-like garment in East Africa especially by the Maasai where it is usually red. The first recorded use of the word in Western literature was by Richard Burton in 1856 in his book "First Footsteps in East Africa."

Tee Tree oil. From the leaves of the Australian tea tree *Melaleuca Alternifolia,* this oil is used to treat acne, cuts, burns, insect bites, fungus and other skin and scalp disorders.

Thoroughbred. A horse breed developed in England in the 18th century by crossing English mares with Arabian stallions to produce a racer. All thoroughbreds are derived from three founding stallions: Darley Arabian, Godolphin Arabian and the Byerly Turk.

Trekboers. Descendants of the original Dutch settlers in the Cape; they began migrating from the areas near Cape Town, Paarl, and Stellenbosch during the 1690s into the eastern Cape and on into what is now Namibia throughout the 1700s.

Warmblood. Any cross between a hot blood such as an Arabian or thoroughbred and a cold blood such as a shire. Typical warmblood breeds include the Dutch Warmblood, Trakehner, and Hanoverian.

Country Descriptions

Botswana

Area: 224,808 square miles
Population: 1,561,973
People: San, Khoe and Tswana
Capital with population: Gabarone. 110,000
Languages:English, Setswana
Religion: Indigenous beliefs, Christian (15%)
Currency: Pula = 100 theba

Kenya

Area: 225,057 square miles
Population: 32,021,856
People: 21% Kikuyu, 14% Lughya,13% Luo, 11% Kamba. 11%Kalenjin, 6% Kisii, 5% Mijikenda, 2%Maasai
Capital with population: Nairobi. 1.5 million.
Languages: Kiswahili, English
Religion: Protestant (19%), Animist (18%), Roman Catholic (27%), Islam (6%).
Currency: Kenya shilling = 100 cents

Malawi

Area: 45,766 square miles
Population: 11, 906,855
People: Chewa, Nyanja, Tumbuko, Yao, Lomwe, Sena, Tonga, Ngoni, Ngonde, Asian, European
Capital with population: Lilongwe, population 230,000
Languages:English, Chichewa
Religion: Protestant 55%, Roman Catholic 20%, Muslim 20%, traditional indigenous beliefs
Currency: Kwatcha = 100 tambala

Namibia

Area: 318,387 square miles
Population: 1,954,033
People: 50% Ovambo tribe and 9% to the Kavangos tribe; other ethnic groups are: Herero 7%, Damara 7%, White 6%, Nama 5%, Caprivian 4%, San 1.5%, Baster 2%, Tswana 0.5%
Capital with population: Windhoek, 150,000
Languages: English 7% (official), Afrikaans common language of most of the population and about 60% of the white population, German 32%, indigenous languages: Oshivambo, Herero, Nama
Religion: Christian 80% to 90%, Lutheran 50% at least, other Christian denominations 30%, native religions 10% to 20%
Currency: South African Rand = 100 cents

South Africa

Area: 471,647 square miles
Population: 42,718,530
People: 76 percent black Africans—Nguni (Zulu, Xhosa, Swazi, Ndebele), Sotho-Tswana, Venda, Tsonga-Shangaan, Khoisan; 13 percent whites—Afrikaners, British, other Europeans; 11 percent Asians and others.
Capital with population: Johannesburg, 3,225,812.
Languages: There are 11 official languages in South Africa: Zulu, Ndebele, Xhosa, N. Sotho, S. Sotho, Tswana, Swazi, Venda, Tsonga, Afrikaans, and English.
Religion: 80% Christian remainder indigenous beliefs and Muslim.
Currency: Rand = 100 cents

Tanzania

Area: 365,056 square miles
Population: 36,588,225
People: native African (95% Bantu, consisting of well over 100 tribes) 99%, Asian, European, and Arab 1%
Capital with population: Dodoma, population 85,000 (legislative) Dar es Salaam (de facto), population 1.1 million
Languages: Kiswahili or Swahili (official), Kiunguju (name for Swahili in Zanzibar), English (official, primary language of commerce, administration, and higher education), Arabic (widely spoken in Zanzibar), many local languages

Religion: Christian 45%, Muslim 35%, indigenous beliefs 20%
Currency: Tanzania shilling = 100 cents

Zambia

Area: 297, 710 square miles
Population: 10,462,436
People: More than 16 different cultural groups
Capital with population: Lusaka, population 985,000
Languages: English (official), major vernaculars—Bemba, Kaonda, Lozi, Lunda, Luvale, Nyanja, Tonga, and about 70 other indigenous languages
Religion: Christian 50%-75%, Muslim and Hindu 24%-49%, indigenous beliefs 1%
Currency: Kwatcha = 100 ngwee

Zimbabwe

Area: 150,937 square miles
Population: 12,671,860
People: African 98% (Shona 71%, Ndebele 16%, other 11%), white 1%, mixed and Asian 1%
Capital with population: Harare, population 680,000
Languages: English (official), Shona, Sindebele (the language of the Ndebele, sometimes called Ndebele), numerous but minor tribal dialects
Religion: Syncretic (part Christian, part indigenous beliefs) 50%, Christian 25%, indigenous beliefs 24%, Muslim and other 1%
Currency: Zimbabwe dollar = 100 cents

Bibliography

Blom, Philipp. *To Have to Hold*. Woodstock: The Overlook Press, 2003.

Buñuel, Luis. *My Last Sigh*. New York: Alfred A. Knopf Incorporated, 1983.

Burton, Richard Francis. *Zanzibar; City Island and Coast*. London: Tinsley Bros., 1872.

Ibid. The Lake Regions of Central Africa; a Picture of Exploration. London: Longmans, 1860.

Culpepper, Nicholas. *The English Physician Enlarged with three hundred and sixty nine medicines made of English herbs*. London: Law, Miller and Catr, 1792.

Dante, Alighieri Trans. By Robert and Jean Hollander. *Inferno* New York: Doubleday, 2000.

Dennett, Daniel. *Darwin's Dangerous Idea. Evolution and the Meanings of Life*. Riverside: Simon & Schuster, 1995.

Dunbar, Robin. *Neocortex size as a constraint on group size in primates*. Journal of Human Evolution Vol. 20, pp. 469-493, 1992.

Eliot, George. *Adam Bede*. Edinburgh & London: William Blackwood and Sons, 1859.

Eliot, T. S. *Four Quartets*. New York: Harcourt, Brace and Company, 1943.

Estes, Richard Despard. *The Safari Companion*. Vermont: Chelsea Green Publishing Company, 1999.

Flaubert, Gustave. Tranlsated by J. Lewis May. *Madame Bovary. A Story of a Provincial Life*. London: John Lane, the Bodley Head, 1928.

Fowler, Henry. *Modern English Usage*. Oxford: Oxford University Press, 1944.

Fox, Paula. *Poor George.* New York: Harcourt, Brace & World, 1967.

Harvey, P. H. and Pagel, M. D. *The comparative method in evolutionary biology.* Oxford: Oxford University Press. 1991.

Huxley, Aldous. *Doors of Perception.* New York: Harper, 1954.

Huxley, Elspeth. *Out in the Mid-day Sun. My Kenya.* London: Chatto & Windus, 1985.

Kipling, Rudyard. *Just So Stories, for Little Children.* London, MacMillan & Co., 1902.

Kruuk, Hans. *The Spotted Hyena.* Chicago: The University Of Chicago Press, 1972.

Leacock Stephen. *Literary Lapses: Reflections on Riding.* Montreal: Gazette Printing Co., 1910.

Leider, Richard, and Shapiro, David. *Repacking Your Bags.* San Francisco: Berrett-Koehler Publishers, Incorporated, 1996.

Ibid. Claiming Your Place at the Fire. Living the second half of your life on purpose. San Francisco: Berrett-Koehler Publishers, Incorporated, 2004.

Madison, James. *Madison to Horatio Gates, February 28, 1794. W.T. Hutchinson et al., The Papers of James Madison, vol. 15, p. 164,* Chicago and Charlottesville, Virginia (1962-1991).

Markham, Beryl. *West with the Night.* Boston: Houghton Mifflin, 1942.

Morris, Donald. *The Washing of the Spears. The rise and fall of the Zulu nation.* New York: Simon & Schuster, 1965.

Muensterberger, Werner. *Collecting: an Unruly Passion.* Princeton University Press: Princeton, 1994.

Pollan, Michael. *Botany of Desire; A Plant's eye view of the world.* London: Bloomsbury Publishing PLC, 2002.

Ibid. Second Nature: A gardener's education. New York: Atlantic Monthly Press, 1991.

Quinn, Daniel. *Ishmael.* New York: Bantam Turner, 1992.

Rood, Betsie. *Smulvleis uit die veld.* Cape Town, Tafelberg, 1977.

Stoker, Bram—*Personal Reminiscences of Henry Irving.* New York: The Macmillan Company, 1906.

Surtees, R. S. *Jorrocks Jaunts and Jollities.* London: Spiers, 1839.

Turle, Gillies. *The Art of the Maasai.* New York: Knopff, 1992.

Van der Post, Lawrence. *The Lost World of the Kalahari.* New York: William Morrow and Company, 1958.

Ibid. Venture to the Interior. London: Hogarth Press, 1952.

978-0-595-37301-7
0-595-37301-1